RUSSIAN MADE EASY
LEVEL 1

An Easy Step-By-Step Approach To Learn Russian for Beginners
(Textbook + Workbook Included)

Lingo Mastery

ISBN: 978-1-951949-66-2

Copyright © 2022 by Lingo Mastery

CONTENTS

FREE BOOK REVEALS THE 6-STEP BLUEPRINT THAT TOOK STUDENTS FROM LANGUAGE LEARNERS TO FLUENT IN 3 MONTHS

✔ 6 Unbelievable Hacks that will accelerate your learning curve

✔ Mind Training: why memorizing vocabulary is easy

✔ One Hack to Rule Them All: This **secret nugget** will blow you away...

Head over to **LingoMastery.com/hacks** and claim your free book now!

INTRODUCTION

Dear reader, if you're holding this book, then you have embarked on a challenging mission to learn the Russian language. Our congratulations to you—Russian is spoken by about 155 million people and it's the eighth most popular language in the world, which makes it an essential tool to widen your horizons in terms of knowledge, business, communication, self-development, and many other things a new language can offer.

Russian people are often said to be unfriendly and even rude. Wrong! This assumption is derived from the fact that they rarely smile and are not very eager to communicate with strangers. However, many people, including scientists, deny the truth of that assumption. The thing is that Russians are really sincere people, and mostly express their emotions when they are strong, deep, and usually directed at someone they know. Once you get to know Russian people better, you'll be surprised by their hospitality and interest in their interlocutor.

The same goes for the Russian language—it can seem hostile and unapproachable, but some time, effort, and diligence will reveal beautiful new ways to express things and look at the world. We're here to help you discover this beauty in a fun, comprehensive, and efficient way.

WHAT DOES THIS BOOK OFFER?

This book is a tool for building and developing vocabulary. However, just knowing many words is not enough to convey things and understand others, which is especially true for the Russian language since it's abundant in endings that are constructed differently, depending on the part of speech and its grammatical characteristics.

Don't get us wrong—we don't mean to intimidate you! In fact, we've arranged vocabulary learning in a way that will let you incorporate the words into your speech and understand them. For this reason, the theoretical part of the book includes:

- Vocabulary lists with translations;
- Set word combinations;
- Ready-to-use conversational formulas and expressions;
- Grammar appendix.

The last point deserves your special attention. Although we've tried to create an out-of-the-box solution and many words are given both in their initial and some widespread forms (like a verb and its form in the 1st person singular), it's impossible to cover all the forms. That is why vocabulary-related information is often interrupted with grammar sections, while more complex grammar rules are covered in a grammar appendix, which we strongly encourage you to use. No overburdening, though, just basic information for you to be able to make grammar changes independently.

The practical part includes exercises with an answer key at the end of the book. In the exercises you will be asked to:

- Choose the correct option;
- Work with images;
- Fill in the blanks;
- Make sentences;
- Match columns;
- Listen to and roleplay conversations;
- Analyze simple texts;
- Ask and answer questions.

The exercises are a mix of conventional drills and more creative, flexible tasks. This way the hard work that is inherent to any language learning process is intertwined with fun, motivating activities that are essential to preserve inspiration and keep going.

The exercises involve different ways of looking at things and promote a change of activities, which ensures better remembering and prevents you from getting bored or discouraged.

HOW TO MAKE THE MOST OUT OF THIS BOOK?

- **Take your time**

We want you to remember that we offer vocabulary and related grammar not for the sake of knowing many rules and words, but for the sake of being able to speak and understand others—efficient communication is our major goal. So, no one expects you to remember all the words, constructions, endings, and peculiarities right away. Feel free to go back to the theory section as many times as needed to look up translations and to see how to make this or that grammatical structure.

- **When doing an exercise, you're not sitting an exam**

The goal of the exercises is to help you remember words and expression lists and to help you understand how things work, so use all the information you have and don't be afraid to make mistakes.

- **Pay attention to the surrounding words**

Even if a sentence is concentrated on some target word you need to use in the right form, for example, make sure you pay attention to the environment. All the sentences are related to the topic, so if you're asked to put the verb 'покупать – to buy' in the correct form, the other words in the sentence will be about buying too. Don't skip them, and take every chance to remember them better.

- **Make sure you get all the value from the conversations**

While many conversations in the book have intentionally missing words or are in the wrong order, filling in blanks and rearranging is not the only thing to do with them. Conversations are full of useful expressions that you can use in real life. So, make sure you act them out and devote enough effort to comparing them with the English translations.

- **Wait before checking the translation**

Many exercises are accompanied by English translations to minimize dictionary consultation and to give you a chance to compare, spot differences, and see how the language works. However, we recommend challenging yourself as much as you can before turning to the translation. The vocabulary used in the exercises is either something you've come across or will be easy to understand from the context.

WHAT VOCABULARY WILL I LEARN IN THIS BOOK?

This book includes the following units:

- *About Myself and My Family;*
- *Daily Activities and Routines;*
- *Traveling and Navigation;*
- *Describing Things;*
- *Buying, Ordering, and Paying.*

You will notice that some units may seem harder and more concentrated in terms of things to remember. This is particularly true for the first two units, because in addition to providing the related vocabulary, they are also focused on giving you the basics of how words are arranged and how they change in different situations. With due diligence and patience, you'll notice that every new unit is easier than the previous one.

Before you plunge into the ocean of the Russian language, here is some wisdom from us—every drop adds up to the wave, so forget about the fact that Russian is one of the most difficult languages in the world and concentrate on the inspiring idea that every new word, mistake, and exercise takes you closer to becoming a confident Russian speaker. Good luck!

BEFORE YOU START

Before you begin expanding your vocabulary and practicing it in exercises, read and analyze the information below. It refers to some peculiarities of the Russian language that make it different from English. Knowing these things will help you get a better idea of how the language functions, as well as how to do the exercises with more ease and efficiency.

THE VERB 'БЫТЬ – TO BE' IN RUSSIAN

⚖ Compare these sentences in Russian and English:

Я пилот – I am a pilot

These sentences mean the same thing, but have a different number of words. The thing is that the Russian verb 'to be – быть' is omitted in the present tense. It makes things easier, doesn't it?

Compare more examples:

Она из Америки. – She is from America.
Они шумные. – They are noisy.
Они мои родители. – They are my parents.
Я врач. – I am a doctor.

TYPES OF SENTENCES AND THEIR WORD ORDER

Affirmative sentences

In the English language, affirmative sentences always follow the Subject (S) + Verb (V) + Object (O) pattern, while in Russian this structure can be rather flexible. The S+V+O pattern is the most widespread one, but you can also come across O+V+S or V+S+O options. The difference between them is the shades of meaning.

Example:

Мы играли в футбол. – We were playing football. – Neutral meaning.
В футбол играли мы. – The same translation with the emphasis on the kind of sport we were playing. That was football and not volleyball or hockey.
Играли мы в футбол. – The emphasis is on the action.

The novelty of information also affects the word order. If it's something new, the word denoting it should be at the end of the sentence, while 'previous' information will go to the beginning.

Завтра мы поедем **в торговый центр.** – We'll go **to the mall** tomorrow.
('Mall' is new information.)
В торговом центре мы купим новую одежду и сходим в кафе. – We'll buy new clothes and go to the café **at the mall**.
(Now 'mall' is known, 'previous' information.)

Conclusion: You can play with word order in affirmative sentences, but whenever you don't feel confident enough, go for the conventional S+V+O structure, and you won't make a mistake.

Negative sentences

There are three particles in Russian that help express negation. They are '**нет**', '**не**', and '**ни**'. All of them require the genitive case of the noun that is negated (see pages 175-177). Let's see what the difference between the particles is.

1) Нет

a) To negate the whole sentence and is most frequently an answer to a question or suggestion

Example:

Ты рано встаёшь по выходным? – **Нет**, по выходным я встаю поздно.
Do you wake up early on weekends? – **No, I don't**. I wake up late on weekends*.
Хочешь чашечку кофе? – **Нет**, спасибо. Я люблю чай.
Would you like a cup of coffee? – **No**, thanks. I like tea.

 *In Russian there is negation and affirmation in one sentence, and this is absolutely normal. First you negate the question about waking up early, and then say that you wake up late in the same sentence.

b) There is no/there are no – absence

The affirmative for there is/are is the verb 'есть'.

Example:

Здесь есть телефон. – There is a telephone here.
В комнате есть врач? – Is there a doctor in the room?
To make a negative sentence, remove 'есть' and add 'нет' with the following noun in the genitive case.

Example:

Здесь **нет** телефона. – There is no phone here.
В комнате **нет** врача. – There is no doctor in the room.

c) Don't have – absence of possession

The pattern is as follows: У + noun or pronoun in the genitive case + нет + noun in the genitive case.

Example:

У меня **нет собаки**. – I don't have a dog.
У папы **нет машины**. – Dad doesn't have a car.

2) He

a) This particle is placed before the part of the sentence that is to be negated and can negate any independent part of speech.

Example:

Я **не** люблю танцевать. – I don't like dancing. (verb)

Эта машина **не** моя. – This car is not mine. (possessive pronoun)

Это **не** книга, это журнал. – This is not a book, this is a magazine. (noun)

Ты **не** говоришь быстро. – You don't talk fast. (adverb)

Дом **не** далеко, а близко. – The house isn't far, but close. (adjective)

b) In double negations (that are the norm in Russian)

Никогда не – never

Ничего не – nothing (accusative, genitive)

Никто не – nobody

Ничто не – nothing

Нигде не – nowhere

Никуда не – nowhere (direction)

Никак не – no way

Example:

Я **никуда не** хожу по выходным. – I go nowhere on weekends.

c) In expressions:

Больше не – no more, not any longer

Ещё не – not yet

Уже не – not any more

Почти не – almost not

Совсем не/нет – not at all

Example:

Я ещё не готов к уроку. – I'm not ready for the lesson yet.

3) Ни

a) Neither ... nor

У неё нет **ни** детей, **ни** мужа. – She has neither kids nor husband.

b) With expressions such as: not a single day, penny, minute – **Ни + noun in genitive case**

Example:

У меня нет **ни минуты** свободного времени. – I don't have a single minute of spare time.

Interrogative sentences

Unlike in English, interrogative sentences in Russian don't require any grammatical change of the sentence. If it's **a question with a question word**, we just add it to the initial affirmative sentence, make the corresponding changes in pronouns, and change the intonation.

For example:

Меня зовут Аня. – The question form of the sentence is: Как тебя зовут?
Мне семь лет. – The question form of the sentence is: Сколько тебе лет?

If it's **a yes/no question,** we simply change the pronoun and the intonation.

For example:

У меня есть семья. – The question form of the sentence is: **У тебя есть семья?**
Я говорю по-немецки. – The question form of the sentence is: **Ты говоришь по-немецки?**

THE DIFFERENCE BETWEEN ТЫ AND ВЫ

Unlike in English, in Russian there are two ways of saying 'you'. 'Ты' is informal and is used when addressing friends and good acquaintances.

'Вы' is formal and is used when we address:

- Older people;
- People of the same age if you don't know each other*;
- Bosses and clients;
- Older relatives*.

Example:

Ты сегодня занята? – Are you busy today? (asking a friend)
Вы можете помочь мне выбрать размер? – Can you help me choose the size? (asking a shop assistant)

 * It's typical to use 'Вы' with all unfamiliar people (like bank workers, passersby, shop assistants, taxi or bus drivers, receptionists, etc.) and with people you are introduced to for the first time.

 ** Children are supposed to use the formal form when addressing all adults outside their family, sometimes including certain family members like aunts, uncles, or their parents' friends. However, in this situation much depends on the relationship. For example, in some families nephews use the informal form to address their uncles, while in others they would say 'Вы'.

ATTRIBUTES OF THE PARTS OF SPEECH AND HOW THEY CORRESPOND TO EACH OTHER

Russian pronouns, nouns, adjectives, and verbs have more grammatical categories than their English counterparts. Moreover, they all should correspond to each other. First, let's see what these categories are.

Pronouns: number, case and gender (the latter only for the 3rd person singular, i.e., 'он/она – he/she).

Nouns: number, gender, and case.

Adjectives: number, gender, and case.

Verb: tense and person (there are three more, but they are not covered in this book for the sake of not overloading you with information).

If parts of speech relate to each other semantically, then they should correspond to each other in all categories, which is reflected in forms and endings.

Example:

Она весёл**ая** девочка.
She's a happy girl.
Nominative case, feminine, singular.

Он весёл**ый** мальчик.
He's a happy boy.
Nominative case, masculine, singular.

The abundance of categories and endings can be rather intimidating, but you'll be given detailed instructions along the way and will always have an opportunity to consult the Grammar Appendix.

HOW TO GET THE AUDIO FILES

Some of the exercises throughout this book come with accompanying audio files.

You can download these audio files if you head over to

www.lingomastery.com/russian-me1-audio

UNIT I
ABOUT MYSELF AND MY FAMILY

This unit includes words and expressions that can help you start a
conversation, give basic information about yourself and your family,
and ask your interlocutor about the same.

VOCABULARY

STARTING A CONVERSATION

🔊 **Saying hello** (Find audio on page 11).

> **Привет!** – Hi! Hello! (informal)
>
> **Здравствуйте!** – Hello! (formal)
>
> **Доброе утро!** – Good morning! (both formal and informal)
>
> **Добрый день!** – Good afternoon! (formal)
>
> **Добрый вечер!** – Good evening! (formal)

🔊 **Informal ways to ask how things are going**

> **Как дела?** – How are you? (informal)
>
> **Как жизнь?** – How's life going? (very informal)
>
> **Как ты? Ты как?** – How are you? What's up? (informal)

🔊 **Formal ways to ask how things are going**

> **Как Ваши дела?** – How are you? (formal)
>
> **Как Вы?** – How are you? How are you doing? (a bit less formal)

📢 **Ways to reply** (Find audio on page 11).
The replies can be preceded by 'Спасибо – Thank you'

> **Очень хорошо** – Very well
>
> **Отлично!** – Great!
>
> **Хорошо** – Fine, well
>
> **Нормально** – Okay
>
> **Неплохо** – Not bad
>
> **Не очень** – Not quite well
>
> **Плохо** – Bad
>
> **Очень плохо** – Very bad

📢 **Note this pattern:**

> **Как дела?** – How are you?
>
> **Хорошо! А у тебя/Вас?** – I'm fine! And you?
>
> **И у меня/тоже хорошо/я тоже хорошо** – I'm fine too.

📢 **Asking back**

> **А у тебя?** – And you? (informal, 2nd person singular)
>
> **А у Вас?** – And you? (formal, 2nd person plural)
>
> **А ты как?** – And you? (very informal, 2nd person singular)

📢 **Saying goodbye**

> **Пока!** – Bye! (informal)
>
> **До свидания!** – Goodbye! (formal)
>
> **(Ну) давай!** – Bye-bye, see you!
>
> **До скорого!** – See you soon! (informal)
>
> **Счастливо!** – Have a good day! (informal)

GIVING INFORMATION ABOUT YOURSELF, YOUR FAMILY, AND FRIENDS

Learning a new language is always associated with learning about a new culture and new people.

We could provide you with a conventional list of the needed vocabulary, but we believe that information we acquire ourselves is easier to memorize. So, first listen to this text in Russian and read its English translation, going paragraph by paragraph. Try to compare the highlighted parts and guess the translations. You will have a chance to check your guesses with the vocabulary list below.

🔊 **Моя семья – My family** (Find audio on page 11).

Привет всем! **Меня зовут** Марина. **Мне двадцать три года. Я из России**. Я хорошо говорю по-английски. Сейчас я живу в Лос-Анджелесе. Я **студентка**. В России у меня большая **семья**. Я скучаю по ней, но здесь **у меня есть друзья.**

Hi everyone! **My name is** Marina. **I'm twenty-three years old. I'm from Russia**. I speak English well. I live in Los Angeles now. I'm a **student**. I have a big **family** in Russia. I miss them, but I have **friends** here.

Моя **подруга** Хэлен. **Ей двадцать один год**. Хелен из Лос-Анджелеса. Она много помогает мне в новом городе. Хелен хочет выучить русский. Я помогаю ей.

My **friend's name is** Helen. **She's twenty-one years old**. Helen is from Los Angeles. She helps me a lot in the new city. Helen wants to learn Russian. I am helping her.

В России у меня есть **мама, папа** и **старший брат**. Моей маме сорок девять лет, а папе пятьдесят три. Мою маму зовут Нина. Она **учительница**. Папу зовут Андрей, он врач. Мои **родители** живут за городом.

In Russia I have a **mom**, a **dad**, and an **elder brother**. My mom is forty-nine years old and my dad is fifty-three. My mother's name is Nina. She's a **teacher**. My father's name is Andrey, he's a **doctor**. My **parents** live in the country.

Мой брат **программист. Его зовут** Артём. **Ему двадцать семь лет**. Сейчас он работает в Германии и отлично говорит по-немецки. Он **женат**. Его **жена** очень милая **девушка. Её зовут** Настя. Ей двадцать пять лет. Она **бухгалтер**. Артём и Настя – замечательная пара! **У них есть ребёнок**. Их **дочка** – моя **племянница** Вика. Ей три года.

My brother is a **programmer. His name is** Artyom. **He's twenty-seven years old**. He works in Germany now and speaks German very well. He's **married**. His **wife** is a very nice **girl. Her name is** Nastya. She's twenty-five years old. She's a **bookkeeper**. Artyom and Nastya are a wonderful couple! They have a **child**. Their **daughter** is my **niece** Vika. She's three years old.

У меня также есть **бабушка** и **дедушка**. Они уже **на пенсии** и любят работать в саду. Они любят, когда их **внуки** приезжают в гости.

I also have a **grandmother** and a **grandfather**. They are already **retired** and like working in the garden. They like it when their **grandchildren** come over for a visit.

А ещё у меня есть **двоюродная сестра**. Она **не замужем**. Её мама – моя тётя. Она очень добрая **женщина** и отлично готовит. Я скучаю по её пирогам, ха-ха. Сейчас мы все не вместе, но у меня скоро каникулы, и я обязательно поеду домой!

I also have a **cousin**. She's **not married**. Her mom is my **aunt**. She's a very kind **woman** and is excellent at cooking. I miss her pies, ha-ha. We're not together now, but I will have holidays soon and I am sure to go home!

📢 FAMILY AND FRIENDS VOCABULARY LIST (Find audio on page 11).

Russian	English	Russian	English
муж	husband	дедушка	granddad
жена	wife	бабушка	grandmother
ребёнок/дети	child/children	родители	parents
дочь/дочка	daughter	девушка	girl/girlfriend
сын	son	парень	guy/boyfriend
мать/мама	mother/mom	племянник	nephew
отец/папа	father/dad	племянница	niece
семья	family	(лучший) друг	(best) friend (male)
старший/младший брат	elder/younger brother	(лучшая) подруга	(best) friend (female)
старшая/младшая сестра	elder/younger sister	женат/замужем	married (male/female)
двоюродный брат	cousin (male)	мужчина	man
двоюродная сестра	cousin (female)	женщина	woman

🔊 PROFESSIONS VOCABULARY LIST (Find audio on page 11).

Russian	English	Russian	English
доктор/врач	doctor (the two words are synonyms)	студент/студентка	student (male/female)
учитель/учительница	teacher (male/female)	водитель	driver
переводчик/переводчица	translator/interpreter (male/female)	ветеринар	vet
юрист	lawyer	медсестра/медбрат	nurse/male nurse
продавец	seller/shop assistant	актёр/актриса	actor/actress
пилот	pilot	фермер	farmer
таксист	taxi driver	спортсмен/спортсменка	sportsman/sportswoman
уборщик/уборщица	cleaner (male/female)	фотограф	photographer
певец/певица	singer (male/female)	пожарный	firefighter
строитель	builder	стюард/стюардесса	flight attendant (male/female)
менеджер	manager	директор	chief manager
пекарь	baker	художник/художница	painter (male/female)
полицейский	police officer	секретарь	secretary
почтальон	mail carrier	учёный	scientist
архитектор	architect	адвокат	attorney

 Important note: The vocabulary lists above mostly feature nouns. Nouns change according to number and gender. See the information on pages 170-172.

🔊 COMMON VERBS VOCABULARY LIST*
(1ST PERSON SINGULAR – I DO) (Find audio on page 11).

Russian	English
Я вижу	I see
Я понимаю	I understand
Я знаю	I know
Я люблю	I like/love
Я жду	I wait (unlike in English, doesn't require a preposition)
Я беру	I take
Я помню	I remember

*These verbs are followed by a noun in the accusative case. See the forms in the Grammar Appendix, pages 179-180.

Example:

Я **жду** своего брата.
I **am waiting** for my brother.

Я **люблю** своих детей.
I **love** my children.

Меня зовут – My name is

Personal pronoun in accusative + зовут + name

Меня зовут Вика. – My name is Vika.

Его зовут Максим. – His name is Maxim.

У меня есть – I've got

У + personal pronoun in genitive + есть + object in nominative

У нас есть дети. – We've got kids.

У меня нет – I don't have

У + personal pronoun in genitive + нет + object in genitive

У неё нет родителей. – She doesn't have parents.

У него нет друзей. – He doesn't have friends.

Мне (не) нравится – I (dis)like

Personal pronoun in dative + (не) нравится

Вам не нравится готовить. – You don't like cooking.

Им нравится танцевать. – They like dancing.

Я из – I'm from

Personal pronoun in nominative + из + country name in genitive*

Она из Италии. – She's from Italy.

Мы из США. – We're from the USA.

*See the forms of country names on page 186

Я говорю по-русски – I speak Russian

Personal pronoun in nominative + по-language name stem + ски*

Она говорит по-английски

*See the forms on page 186

Я знаю английский – I know English*

*See languages names and their forms on page 186

Мне ... лет (года, год) – I'm ... old

Personal pronoun in dative + cardinal numeral + лет, года, or год

Мне двадцать один год. – I'm twenty-one years old.

Ему тридцать три года. – He's thirty-three years old.

HOW TO DIFFERENTIATE BETWEEN ЛЕТ/ГОДА/ГОД WHEN TALKING ABOUT AGE?

The word depends on the number.

Number	Word	Example
1 and numbers that end with 1	Год	Ей 51 год. – She's 51 years old.
2, 3, 4 and numbers that end with 2, 3, 4	Года	Ему 74 года. – He's 74 years old.
Numbers from 5 to 19, number 0, numbers ending in 5-19 and 0	Лет	Мне 10 лет. – I'm 10 years old.

Number	Spelling
1	один
2	два
3	три
4	четыре
5	пять
6	шесть
7	семь
8	восемь
9	девять
10	десять
11	одиннадцать
12	двенадцать
13	тринадцать
14	четырнадцать
15	пятнадцать
16	шестнадцать
17	семнадцать
18	восемнадцать
19	девятнадцать

20	двадцать
21, 22, 27…	двадцать один, двадцать два, двадцать семь…
30	тридцать
40	сорок
50	пятьдесят
60	шестьдесят
70	семьдесят
80	восемьдесят
90	девяносто
100	сто
101, 108, 109 …	сто один, сто восемь, сто девять…
200	двести
300	триста
400	четыреста
500	пятьсот
600	шестьсот
700	семьсот
800	восемьсот
900	девятьсот
1000	тысяча
1000000	миллион
1000000000	миллиард

🔊 PERSONAL AND POSSESSIVE PRONOUNS (Find audio on page 11).

Just like in English, there are personal and possessive pronouns in Russian*. Possessive pronouns indicate belonging to somebody or something.

Personal pronoun	Possessive pronoun
Я – I	Мой – My
Ты – You	Твой – Your
Мы – We	Наш – Our
Вы – You	Ваш – Your
Он – He	Его – His
Она – She	Её – Her
Оно – It	Его – Its
Они – They	Их – Their

Example:

Я студент. У меня есть брат. Это **мой** брат. – I'm a student. I have a brother. This is **my** brother.

*Both types of pronouns change according to number, gender, and case. See the forms in the Grammar Appendix (pages 173-174).

Мой дом
My house
Singular, masculine

Моя сестра
My sister
Singular, feminine

Мои родственники
My relatives
Plural

Pronouns 'его', 'её', and 'их' coincide in all number, gender, and case forms.

Example:

Это её дочь. – This is her daughter. (Nominative, singular, feminine)

Это её сын. – This is her son. (Nominative, singular, masculine)

Это её дети. – These are her children. (Nominative, plural)

Я знаю её дочь. – I know her daughter. (Accusative, singular, feminine)

Я знаю её детей. – I know her children. (Accusative, plural)

 Possessive pronouns for 'он', 'она', 'оно', and 'они' correspond to the forms of these personal pronouns in the accusative case.

Example:

Я знаю его. – I know him. (Accusative)

Это его сын. – This is his son. (Possessive)

 When pronouns 'он, она, оно, они' are preceded by a preposition, the spelling is changed and the letter 'н' is added.

For example:

Мы идём **без него**. – We're going **without him**.

 Pronoun '**оно**' requires special attention. Unlike the English 'it', this pronoun does not necessarily indicate an inanimate object or animal. Instead, it's used to replace nouns in neutral gender.

Example:

Солнце уже встало. Оно яркое. – The sun has risen. It is bright.

Какое красивое животное! Оно такое большое! – What a beautiful animal! It is so big!

 Unlike in English, there is no differentiation between 'my' and 'mine', so there is one Russian pronoun for both cases.

Example:

Это мой дом. – This is my house.

Этот дом мой. – This house is mine.

📢 POSSESSIVE PRONOUNS IN SINGULAR AND PLURAL

Singular	Plural
Мой – My	Мои
Твой – Your	Твои
Наш – Our	Наши
Ваш – Your	Ваши
Его – His	Его
Её – Her	Её
Его – Its	Его
Их – Their	Их

Note that some singular and plural forms coincide.

For example:

Это **твои** дети. – These are **your** kids.

Я знаю **его**. Это **его** сын. – I know **him**. This is **his** son.

PRONOUN 'СВОЙ'*

Pronoun 'свой' usually causes confusion among foreigners who learn Russian, since there is no corresponding pronoun in English, nor in many other languages.

This reflexive pronoun is used instead of a possessive pronoun when we need to refer an object to the subject of the sentence, i.e., to the doer of the action.

Example:

Он любит **свой** дом. – He likes **his** house.

In this case, we use the pronoun 'свой' because the object (the house) belongs to the subject (he).

However, if an object belongs to some other person or object, then we should use a regular possessive pronoun.

Example:

Я иду в гости к Андрею. Это **его** дом. – I'm going to visit Andrew. This is **his** house.

Grammar note:

With the 1st and 2nd person you can use either the pronoun 'свой' or the corresponding possessive pronoun.

Example:

Покажи мне **твой/свой** дом. – Show me your house.

Я крашу **мой/свой** дом. – I am painting my house.

Remember, with the 3rd person the differentiation between the reflexive and the possessive pronoun is obligatory.

 Unlike in English, there is no need to use a possessive pronoun when talking about body parts. The same refers to talking about relatives.

Compare:

Я чищу зубы. – I'm brushing **my** teeth.

Я живу с родителями. – I live with **my** parents.

*This pronoun changes according to number, gender, and case. See the Grammar Appendix for the forms (page 174).

Кто это?	Who is it?
Как тебя зовут?	What is your name?
Какая у тебя фамилия?	What is your last name?
Сколько тебе лет?	How old are you?
Откуда ты?	Where are you from?
Кто ты по профессии?	What do you do (for a living)? What's your profession?
У тебя есть семья?	Do you have a family?
Ты говоришь по-английски?	Do you speak English?

📢 The 'Как тебя зовут?' question is associated with getting introduced to new people. So, let's see **how to say you are pleased to meet someone.**

(Очень) приятно познакомиться!	(Very) pleased to meet you!
Взаимно!	The pleasure is mine!
И мне приятно познакомиться!	Pleased to meet you too!
И мне!	Me too!

These questions are based on the pronoun 'ты'. In the exercises section you will have a chance to practice these questions with the other pronouns.

📝 Exercises

📢 **01.** Listen to these short conversations and fill in the missing words.

Conversation 1

A: Привет!

B: _Привет!_____!

A: Как дела?

B: _хорошо, а у тебя_____.

A: _N у меня_____

Conversation 2

A: _Здравствуйте_____!

B: Добрый день!

A: _____?

B: Спасибо, хорошо! _____?

A: Я тоже хорошо!

Conversation 3

A: Привет! Как _____?

B: Привет! Отлично! _____?

A: _____!

Conversation 4

A: _____!

B: Доброе утро!

A: _____?

B: _____, неплохо! _____?

A: Я _____!

02. Complete the family tree with the missing names of relatives.

1) _____.

2) _____.

3) _____.

4) _____.

5) _____.

6) _____.

7) _____.

8) _____.

03. Complete the table with the words from 'Моя семья' text that are antonyms either in gender or number. See the example.

Example: Муж (husband) – Жена (wife)

не женат – not married (about males)	
студент – student (male)	
сестра – sister	
мама и папа – mom and dad	
его зовут – his name is	
парень – guy, young man	
дети – children, kids	
не замужем – not married (about females)	
один друг – one friend	
племянник – nephew	
внук и внучка – grandson and granddaughter	
двоюродный брат – cousin (male)	
дядя – uncle	
мужчина – man	
друг – male friend	
сын – son	

04. Write the translation for these phrases.

1) Меня зовут _____.

2) Её зовут _____.

3) Его зовут _____.

4) У меня есть _____.

5) У них есть _____.

6) Мне двадцать три года _____.

7) Ей двадцать один год _____.

8) Ему двадцать семь лет _____.

05. Take a look at these images and match them with the phrases that define people's names.

A) Masha and Sveta

B) Nastya and Olya

C) Bogdan and Valera

D) Vera

E) Igor Vladimirovich

(   ) **1)** Их зовут Настя и Оля

(   ) **2)** Нас зовут Маша и Света

(   ) **3)** Вас зовут Богдан и Валера

(   ) **4)** Вас зовут Игорь Владимирович

(   ) **5)** Тебя зовут Вера

06. Match the Russian and the English ways of talking about people's names.

Russian	English
( ) **1)** Его зовут Саша	**A)** Her name is Snezhana
( ) **2)** Тебя зовут Лиза	**B)** My name is Katya
( ) **3)** Нас зовут Женя и Егор	**C)** Their names are Sonya and Vlada
( ) **4)** Меня зовут Катя	**D)** Your name is Liza
( ) **5)** Их зовут Соня и Влада	**E)** Our names are Zhenya and Yegor
( ) **6)** Вас зовут мистер Джонсон	**F)** Your names are Danila and Ilya
( ) **7)** Её зовут Снежана	**G)** His name is Sasha
( ) **8)** Вас зовут Данила и Илья	**H)** Your name is Mr. Johnson

07. Fill in the blanks with correct pronouns to make 'My name' phrases. See the example and try to create similar phrases about your relatives.

Example: У меня есть брат. _____зовут Лёня. – I have a brother. His name is Lyonya.

1) У меня есть бабушка. _____зовут Люба.

2) У меня есть друзья. _____зовут Паша и Сергей.

3) У меня есть муж. _____зовут Коля.

4) У меня есть дети. _____зовут Таня и Лера.

5) У меня есть тётя. _____зовут Наташа.

6) У меня есть родители. _____зовут Лида и Антон.

7) У меня есть папа. _____зовут Степан.

8) У меня есть старший брат. _____зовут Игорь.

08. Fill in the correct pronoun in the nominative case. Try to guess the names of professions that are highlighted in bold.

1) Меня зовут Женя. _____**архитектор**.

_____ .

2) Его зовут Матвей. _____**водитель**.

_____ .

3) Их зовут Максим и Влад. _____**друзья**.

_____ .

4) Вас зовут Аркадий Иванович. _____**профессор**.

_____ .

5) Её зовут Таня. _____**учительница**.

_____ .

6) Его зовут Миша. _____**продавец**.

_____.

7) Его зовут Паша. _____**пилот**.

_____.

8) Её зовут Лена. _____**художница**.

_____.

9) Тебя зовут Коля. _____**юрист**.

_____.

09. Fill in the right form of the pronoun in the accusative case. Remember the translations of the highlighted verbs and check your work with the vocabulary section, if needed.

1) Мой ребёнок играет рядом. Я **вижу** _____ .

2) Ты хорошо говоришь по-английски. Я **понимаю** _____ .

3) Это мои родственники. Я **знаю** _____ .

4) Это моя жена. Я **люблю** _____ .

5) Вы мои пациенты. Я **жду** _____ .

6) Это хорошие туфли (shoes). Я **беру** _____ .

7) Вы мой клиент. Я **помню** _____ .

8) Вы мой учитель. Я **знаю** _____ .

10. Make sentences according to the example. Pay attention to the genitive case of the pronouns.

Example: Я/семья – У меня есть семья.

1) Мы/сестра _____ .

2) Он/жена _____ .

3) Вы/дети _____ .

4) Он/бабушка _____ .

5) Вы/сын _____ .

6) Она/подруга _____ .

7) Они/племянница _____ .

8) Мы/дом _____ .

9) Я/собака _____ .

10) Ты/дочка _____ .

11. Complete the sentences below with the correct forms of the dative case. See pages (177-179), if needed.

Example: (Я) 55 лет. – Мне 55 лет.

       (Она) нравится петь. – Ей нравится петь.

1) (Она) 16 лет. _____ .

2) Я) нравится рисовать. _____ .

3) (Они) не нравится плавать. _____ .

4) (Мы) 65 лет. _____ .

5) (Ты) нравится петь. _____ .

6) (Он) нравится смотреть фильмы. _____ .

7) (Вы) не нравится играть в футбол. _____ .

8) (Ты) 43 года. _____ .

9) (Она) нравится играть на гитаре. _____ .

10) (Вы) нравится путешествовать. _____ .

12. Use the correct form of the pronoun and spell out the numbers. Pay attention to the correct use of the words год/года/лет.

Example: Ты/27 – Тебе двадцать семь лет.

1) Я/34 _____ .

2) Мы/20 _____ .

3) Он/45 _____ .

4) Она/51 _____ .

5) Ты/69 _____ .

6) Они/5 _____ .

7) Она/103 _____ .

8) Вы/16 _____ .

9) Я/70 _____ .

10) Он/84 _____ .

13. Complete 'I like' phrases according to the example. Try to guess the meaning of the verbs based on the images.

Example: (Я) / нравится готовить. – Мне нравится готовить (I like to cook / I like cooking).

1) (Она) / нравится танцевать.

_____.

2) (Я) / нравится бегать.

_____.

3) (Они) / не нравится петь.

_____.

4) (Ты) / нравится рисовать.

_____.

5) (Он) / нравится петь.

_____.

6) (Вы) / нравится играть на гитаре.

_____

7) (Мы) / нравится путешествовать.

_____

8) (Я) / не нравится плавать.

_____

9) (Вы) / нравится играть в футбол.

_____

10) (Ты) / нравится кататься на велосипеде.

_____

14. Match the sentences with the images, adjust the words in brackets using the corresponding form of the possessive pronoun, and write down the sentences in the lines below.

Example: Это (я) дедушка. – Это мой дедушка. – This is my grandfather.

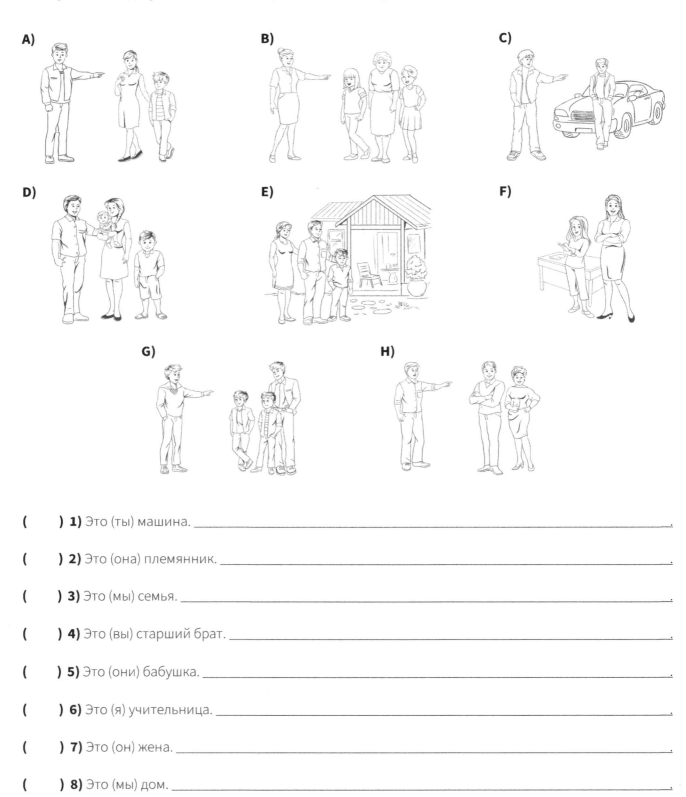

A)

B)

C)

D)

E)

F)

G)

H)

(   ) **1)** Это (ты) машина. _____.

(   ) **2)** Это (она) племянник. _____.

(   ) **3)** Это (мы) семья. _____.

(   ) **4)** Это (вы) старший брат. _____.

(   ) **5)** Это (они) бабушка. _____.

(   ) **6)** Это (я) учительница. _____.

(   ) **7)** Это (он) жена. _____.

(   ) **8)** Это (мы) дом. _____.

15. Match the questions with their English translations and answers.

Question	Translation	Answer
1) Как тебя зовут?	( ) **A)** Where are you from?	( ) **a)** Мне тридцать лет.
2) Откуда ты?	( ) **B)** What is your profession?	( ) **b)** Меня зовут Аня.
3) Сколько тебе лет?	( ) **C)** What is your name?	( ) **c)** Я переводчица.
4) У тебя есть семья?	( ) **D)** How old are you?	( ) **d)** Я из России.
5) Кто ты по профессии?	( ) **E)** Do you have a family?	( ) **e)** Да, у меня есть семья.

16. Complete these conversations with the answers from the list, and then answer these questions yourself, where applicable.

a) Это моя подруга Света.

b) Да, это мои мама и папа.

c) Да, у меня есть брат.

d) Да, я говорю по-английски.

e) Да, я ваш учитель.

f) Её фамилия Великанова.

g) Ему одиннадцать лет.

h) Мама — актриса, а папа — бухгалтер.

i) Я из Турции.

I

Q: У тебя есть брат или сестра?

A: 1) _____ .

Q: Сколько ему лет?

A: 2) _____ .

II

Q: Кто это?

A: 1) _____ .

Q: Какая у неё фамилия?

A: 2) _____ .

III

Q: Это твои родители?

A: 1) _____ .

Q: Кто они по профессии?

A: 2) _____ .

IV

Q: Вы наш учитель?

A: 1) _____ .

Q: Откуда вы?

A: 2) _____ .

V

Q: Ты говоришь по-английски?

A: 1) _____ .

17. Fill in the conversations. After checking your work with the answer key, listen and repeat after the speaker, then roleplay them.

Conversation 1

A: Привет!

B: Привет! Как тебя _____?

A: _____зовут Вика.

B: Очень приятно! А меня зовут Степан.

A: _____ты?

B: Я _____России. А ты?

A: _____из Украины. _____тебе лет?

B: Мне двадцать один _____. А тебе?

Conversation 2

A: У тебя _____семья?

B: Да, у _____есть семья. У меня есть сестра Лена.

A: Сколько _____лет?

B: Ей тридцать четыре _____.

A: _____она?

B: Она _____России.

A: У _____есть семья?

B: Да, она замужем.

Conversation 3

A: Здравствуйте! Как _____зовут?

B: Меня _____Валерий Петрович.

A: Сколько _____лет?

B: Мне сорок _____.

A: Кто _____по профессии?

B: _____врач.

18. Insert the words from the boxes into the texts. After checking your work with the answer key, listen and repeat after the speaker.

Text 1

> зовут испанский лет меня по-русски Аргентины нас
> учительница замужем из ему пять мне мы есть его

1) _____ зовут Анна. **2)** _____ 30 лет. Я **3)** _____ Испании. Я работаю в школе.

Я **4)** _____. Я преподаю **5)** _____. Я также умею говорить

6) _____.

Я **7)** _____. Мой муж архитектор. **8)** _____ 32 года. Он из **9)** _____.

Его **10)** _____ Хулио.

У **11)** _____ есть двое детей – Мари и Эстебан. Мари 8 **12)** _____, а Эстебану - 6. У нас **13)** _____

собака. **14)** _____ зовут Пушок. Ему **15)** _____ лет. **16)** _____ счастливая (happy) семья!

Text 2

> девушка замужем мой на зовут моя по-английски года
> их её ему моя меня его

Меня **1)** _____ Антонина. Мне шестьдесят четыре **2)** _____. Я **3)** _____ пенсии. Я не

4) _____. **5)** _____ сестра Наташа живёт в Украине. **6)** _____ дети – мои племянники.

Старшего зовут Максим. **7)** _____ двадцать пять лет. Он хорошо говорит **8)** _____

и по-немецки. У него есть **9)** _____. Она переводчица. **10)** _____ младший племянник

ещё студент. **11)** _____ зовут Игорь. У **12)** _____ нет детей, но у меня очень хорошие

племянники. Я очень люблю **13)** _____.

Text 3

> его России танцевать нам женат моя нравится есть своя

Это Марина. Она **1)** _____ лучшая подруга. Мы из **2)** _____. Сейчас мы живём в

Италии. Мы студентки. **3)** _____ девятнадцать лет. Марина очень активная девушка. Ей нравится

4) _____ и плавать. В Италии у неё **5)** _____ двоюродный брат. Он **6)** _____.

У него есть **7)** _____ семья. **8)** _____ жена художница. Мне тоже **9)** _____ рисовать.

19. Listen to the texts and place a check mark in the correct column. Tell us much as you can about these people and then write down the sentences. Finally, try to make similar sentences about yourself.

	Лера	Франц	Костя	Грэг
студент(ка)				
продавец				
актёр				
водитель				
плавать				
рисовать				
играть в футбол				
путешествовать				
женат				
замужем				
не женат				
не замужем				
есть дети				
нет детей				
из России				
из Германии				
из Америки				
по-русски				
по-немецки				
по-английски				
по-турецки				

20. Look through these forms and make small texts. Follow the sample. Then fill in the last form and write a text about yourself.

Sample:

Имя/Name: Макар

Фамилия/Surname: Сахаров

Возраст/Age: 54

Страна/Country: Россия

Профессия/Profession: Маркетолог

Языки/Languages: Английский, русский, немецкий

Замужем/женат/Married: Да

Дети/Children: Да

Его зовут Макар Сахаров. Ему 54 года. Он из России. Он маркетолог. Он говорит по-английски, по-русски и по-немецки. Он женат. У него есть дети.

А)

Имя/Name: Жули

Фамилия/Surname: Решар

Возраст/Age: 18

Страна/Country: Франция

Профессия/Profession: Студентка

Языки/Languages: Английский, французский

Замужем/женат/Married: Нет

Дети/Children: Нет

_____

_____

_____ .

B)

Имя/**Name:** Рикардо

Фамилия/**Surname:** Феллини

Возраст/**Age:** 27

Страна/**Country:** Италия

Профессия/**Profession:** Юрист

Языки/**Languages:** Английский, итальянский

Замужем/женат/**Married:** Да

Дети/**Children:** Да

_____

_____

_____.

C)

Имя/**Name:** _____

Фамилия/**Surname:** _____

Возраст/**Age:** _____

Страна/**Country:** _____

Профессия/**Profession:** _____

Языки/**Languages:** _____

Замужем/женат/**Married:** _____

Дети/**Children:** _____

_____

_____

_____.

UNIT II
EVERYDAY ACTIVITIES
AND ROUTINES

This unit includes words, expressions, and grammar that you will need to talk about what you do every day, what you like and dislike, how you spend your free time and working hours. You will learn how to discuss these things with other people and ask questions about these routines.

VOCABULARY

In order to avoid passive (and inefficient) learning, read this text and compare it with the English translation, paragraph by paragraph, to guess the meaning of the new words and gradually check your answers with the vocabulary lists below.

📣 Мой день – My day

Привет! Меня зовут Валентин. Я бухгалтер. **По будням я просыпаюсь в 6 утра**. Я **умываюсь, чищу зубы, бреюсь** и быстро **завтракаю**. Мне не нравится завтракать, но я знаю – **это важно**. Я **не делаю утреннюю зарядку. У меня нет на это времени!** Затем я одеваюсь и **выхожу из дома** в 6:40.

Hi! My name is Valentin. I'm a bookkeeper. **On weekdays I wake up at 6 a.m**. I **wash, brush my teeth, shave,** and **have breakfast** quickly. I don't like having breakfast, but I know **it's important**. I **don't do any morning exercises. I don't have time for that! Then I get dressed** and **leave home** at 6:40 a.m.

Мой офис **далеко от** дома. **У меня нет машины**. Я **езжу на работу на автобусе. Иногда я опаздываю,** тогда я **беру такси. Я всегда приезжаю на работу вовремя. Мой рабочий день начинается ровно в** 8 утра.

My office is **far from** my house. I **don't have a car**. I **go to work by bus. Sometimes I run late**, so I **take a taxi. I always get to work on time. My working day starts at** 8 a.m. **sharp**.

У меня **обеденный перерыв с** 13:00 **до** 14:00. Я **не беру обед с собой**. У меня нет времени его готовить. Я обедаю **в столовой. Иногда мы с коллегами ходим в кафе**. Мой рабочий день **заканчивается** в 17:00. Я **часто возвращаюсь домой пешком**. У меня есть время **подумать** или **поговорить по телефону** с друзьями.

I have **a lunch break from** 1 p.m. **till** 2 p.m. I **don't take lunch with me**. I don't have time to make it. I have lunch **at the cafeteria. Sometimes my colleagues and I go to the café**. My working day **ends** at 5 p.m. I **often go back home on foot**. I have time to **think** or **talk** to my friends **on the phone**.

Иногда **после работы** я **навещаю своих родителей**. Мама готовит вкусный **ужин. Два раза в неделю** после работы я **хожу в спортзал. Я люблю** спорт! Вечером я обычно смотрю телевизор или **читаю**. Я **никогда не ложусь спать рано**. Я знаю – это неправильно. **Обычно я засыпаю в 12 – 1:30 ночи**.

Sometimes I **visit my parents after work**. Mom cooks a delicious **dinner. Twice a week** after work **I go to the gym. I love sports! In the evening I usually watch TV** or **read**. I **never go to bed early**. I know it's not right. **I usually fall asleep at 12 – 1:30 a.m**.

По выходным я просыпаюсь в 10 – 11 часов утра. Я люблю поспать! В субботу мне нравится активный отдых. Мы с друзьями ходим в кино, ездим на экскурсии, ходим в походы. По воскресеньям я люблю оставаться дома. Иногда мне нужен пассивный отдых. Я смотрю фильмы, заказываю еду и иногда сплю днём. Рабочая неделя, я готов!

On weekends I wake up at 10 – 11 a.m. I love sleeping! On Saturdays I like active relaxation. My friends and I go to the cinema, go on excursions, or go hiking. On Sundays I like staying at home. Sometimes I need passive relaxation. I watch movies, order food, and sometimes sleep during the daytime. Then I'm ready to start my working week!

📣 DAILY ROUTINES VOCABULARY LIST

Note, all the verbs are given in their initial form, followed by the 1st person singular form (I do) for your convenience. See the Grammar Appendix pages 186-189 to use these verbs in other forms.

Russian	English
просыпаться/просыпаюсь	wake up
вставать/встаю	get up
умываться/умываюсь	wash
бриться/бреюсь	shave
чистить/чищу зубы	brush teeth/brush my teeth
принимать/принимаю душ	take a shower
готовить/готовлю завтрак	make breakfast
завтракать/завтракаю	have breakfast
выгуливать/выгуливаю собаку	walk the dog
бегать/бегаю	go jogging
делать/делаю утренние упражнения	do morning exercises
одевать/одеваю детей	dress the kids
одеваться/одеваюсь	get dressed
выходить/выхожу из дома	leave home
отвозить/отвожу детей в садик, школу	take the kids to kindergarten, school
работать/работаю из дома	work from home
идти/иду на работу	go to work
учиться/учусь в университете, школе	study at university, school

ехать/еду на работу	go to work (by vehicle)
рабочий день начинается в…	working day starts at…
приходить/прихожу вовремя	arrive on time
опаздывать/опаздываю	run late or be late
обедать/обедаю	have lunch
ходить/хожу в буфет, столовую, кафе	go to the buffet, cafeteria, café
просматривать/просматриваю почту	go through the emails
ходить/хожу на совещания	go to meetings
отвечать/отвечаю на звонки	answer the phone
рабочий день заканчивается в…	the working day ends at…
возвращаться/возвращаюсь домой	go back home
говорить/говорю по телефону	talk on the phone
встречаться/встречаюсь с	meet somebody
приходить/прихожу домой	come home
у меня есть время на это	I have time for it
у меня нет времени на это	I don't have time for it
забирать/забираю детей из садика, школы	pick up the kids from kindergarten, school
раздеваться/раздеваюсь	undress
ужинать/ужинаю	have dinner
смотреть/смотрю телевизор	watch TV
читать/читаю	read
ходить/хожу на прогулку, в спортзал	go for a walk, to the gym
играть/играю в компьютерные игры	play computer games
убирать/убираю дома; заниматься/занимаюсь уборкой; делать/делаю уборку	clean the house, do the cleaning
укладывать/укладываю детей спать	put the kids to bed
принимать/принимаю ванну	take a bath
заводить/завожу будильник	set the alarm clock
ложиться/ложусь спать	go to bed
засыпать/засыпаю	fall asleep

🔊 ASKING AND ANSWERING QUESTIONS ABOUT DAILY ROUTINES

Question	Sample Answer
Во сколько ты обычно просыпаешься по будням? At what time do you usually wake up on weekdays?	**Обычно я просыпаюсь в семь утра.** I usually wake up at seven a.m.
Ты завтракаешь? Do you have breakfast? **Что ты обычно ешь на завтрак?** What do you usually have for breakfast?	**Я редко завтракаю.** I rarely have breakfast. **Обычно я ем на завтрак овсяную кашу.** I usually have oats for breakfast.
Во сколько ты выходишь из дома? At what time do you leave home?	**Я выхожу из дома в половину восьмого.** I leave home at half past seven.
Как ты добираешься до работы? How do you get to work?	**Я добираюсь до работы на метро.** I get to work by subway.
Ты берёшь обед с собой? Do you take lunch with you?	**Нет, я обедаю в столовой.** No, I don't. I have lunch at the canteen.
Во сколько начинается/заканчивается твой рабочий день? When does your working day start/end?	**Мой рабочий день начинается в девять утра.** My working day starts at nine a.m.
Во сколько ты возвращаешься домой после работы? At what time do you get back home after work?	**Я возвращаюсь домой в шесть вечера.** I get back home at six p.m.
Что ты обычно делаешь (чем ты занимаешься) после работы? What do you usually do after work?	**После работы я обычно читаю или встречаюсь с друзьями.** After work I usually read or meet my friends.
В котором часу ты ложишься спать? At what time do you go to bed?	**Я ложусь спать в одиннадцать часов.** I go to bed at eleven o'clock.
Чем ты занимаешься на выходных? What do you do at weekends?	**На выходных я провожу время с семьёй.** At weekends I spend my time with family.
Тебе больше нравятся активные или пассивные выходные? Do you like active or passive weekends more?	**Мне больше нравятся активные выходные.** I like active weekends more.

TIME PERIODS

Russian	English
секунда	second
минута	minute
час	hour
день	day
неделя	week
месяц	month
год	year

WORDS OF FREQUENCY

Russian	English
всегда	always
почти всегда	almost always
иногда	sometimes
обычно	usually
редко	rarely, seldom
очень редко	very rarely
каждый день/вечер/месяц/год	every day/evening/month/year
каждую ночь/неделю	every night/week
каждое утро/воскресенье	every morning/Sunday
никогда не	never
почти никогда не	almost never

 Unlike in English, double negation is normal in Russian. For example, take the 'никогда' adverb. Although this word has a negative meaning, the verb still needs particle 'не' to form negation.

Example: Я **никогда не** делаю утреннюю гимнастику. – I **never** do morning exercises.

THE POSITION OF FREQUENCY ADVERBS IN THE SENTENCE

> Часто, редко, всегда, никогда не + Verb

Example: Я **часто** готовлю завтрак. – I **often** make breakfast.

Я **редко** опаздываю. – I am **rarely** late.

Я **всегда** прихожу вовремя. – I **always** come on time.

Я **никогда не** завожу будильник. – I **never** set the alarm clock.

> Иногда, обычно + Verb
>
> or
>
> Verb + Иногда, обычно

Example: Обычно я просыпаюсь в 7 утра. – I usually wake up at 7 a.m.

Я **обычно** просыпаюсь в 7 утра.

Иногда я работаю из дома. – Sometimes I work from home.

Я **иногда** работаю из дома.

> **Каждый день (год, и т.д.)***
>
> A) At the beginning of the sentence
>
> B) Before the verb
>
> C) At the end of the sentence

Example: Каждый день я хожу на работу. – I go to work every day.

Я **каждый день** хожу на работу.

Я хожу на работу **каждый день**.

*The word 'каждый' changes according to the gender of the noun it relates to. See the Grammar Appendix for the rule (page 185).

QUESTIONS FOR FREQUENCY ADVERBS

You can ask yes/no questions with frequency adverbs. Here is the pattern:

> Subject + frequency adverb + verb

For example: Ты **часто** ходишь в спортзал? – Do you **often** go to the gym?

Ты **всегда** приходишь вовремя? – Do you **always** come on time?

> Как часто? – How often?

You can also ask a special question:

Example: Как часто ты делаешь утреннюю гимнастику? – **How often** do you do morning exercises?

Here are the ways to answer this question:

> Каждый + time period (e.g. day) – Every day
>
> Number + раз + в + time period – Once a day

Example: Как часто ты убираешь дома? – **How often** do you clean the house?

Я убираю дома **один раз в неделю**. – I clean the house **once a week**.

Как часто ты работаешь из дома? – **How often** do you work from home?

Я работаю из дома **каждый день**. – I work from home **every day**.

Note that the word 'раз' – 'time' can change depending on the numeral it's preceded by:

> 2, 3, 4, and numerals ending in 2, 3, 4 (except for 12, 13, 14) + раз**а**

For example: Я гуляю с собакой **четыре раза** в неделю.

I walk my dog **four times** a week.

Я просматриваю почту **пять раз** в день.

I go through the mail **five times** a day.

 **DAYS OF THE WEEK – ДНИ НЕДЕЛИ**

Russian	English
понедельник/по понедельникам	Monday/on Mondays
вторник/по вторникам	Tuesday/on Tuesdays
среда/по средам	Wednesday/on Wednesdays
четверг/по четвергам	Thursday/on Thursdays
пятница/по пятницам	Friday/on Fridays
суббота/по субботам	Saturday/on Saturdays
воскресенье/по воскресеньям	Sunday/on Sundays

 Memorizing tip:

'Неделя' is the Russian for 'week' and 'по**недель**ник' starts the week. Yes, Russians start their weeks on Mondays and not on Sundays.

'Второй' is the Russian for 'second', so it corresponds to the second day of the week.

'Четверг' and 'пятница' resemble numbers 'четыре' (4) and 'пять' (5), which corresponds to their order in the week.

USEFUL EXPRESSIONS WITH THE DAYS OF THE WEEK

Каждое воскресенье – Every Sunday
В субботу – On Saturday

 For the sake of convenience, preposition 'в' is replaced with 'во' when used with the word 'вторник'. Otherwise, there would be three consonants in a row, which could cause stumbling even for native speakers.

Во вторник – On Tuesday

TELLING THE TIME IN RUSSIAN

When telling the time, Russians can use two different approaches.

A) 24-hour time.

In this case they don't use a.m. or p.m., because this information comes from the numbers: 00:00-12:00 is a.m. and 13:00-24:00 is p.m.

B) 12-hour time + the words утра, дня, вечера, ночи.

These words can be considered the Russian equivalent for a.m. and p.m. Which time periods apply to which word?

1) 0:00 – 6:00 a.m. – ночи (in the night)
2) 6:00 a.m. – 12:00 p.m. – утра (in the morning)
3) 12:00 a.m. – 6:00 p.m. – дня (in the day)
4) 6:00 p.m. – 12:00 p.m. – вечера (in the evening)

Note that this divide is approximate and much depends on personal perception. For example, if a person wakes up at 4:00 a.m., they will likely use the word 'утра' – 'in the morning', because waking up is associated with this part of the day. So, this rule is quite flexible.

TELLING EXACT TIME (WITHOUT MINUTES)

The main word for this is **'час' – 'hour'** and can have different forms, depending on the numeral.

a) 1, 21 – Час
b) 2, 3, 4, 22, 23, and 24 – Час**а**
c) 5-20 – Час**ов**

Example: Ways of saying 'It's 7 p.m. now':

Сейчас семь вечера.
Сейчас семь часов вечера.
Сейчас девятнадцать часов вечера.

 You can even say: 'Сейчас семь', if the situation makes it clear which part of the day it is now.

 As you noticed, the word 'часов' and its forms can be omitted. However, with numerals after twelve it's less typical. Compare:

Сейчас десять. – Сейчас пятнадцать часов.
It's ten o'clock now. – It's 3 p.m. now.

The word **'ровно'** is the Russian equivalent for **'exactly/sharp'** in the context of telling the time. It can be placed either before the numeral or at the end of the sentence.

Example: Сейчас **ровно** два часа ночи. – It's **exactly** 2 a.m. now.

Сейчас два часа ночи **ровно**.

TELLING THE TIME WITH MINUTES

The easiest way to tell the time with minutes is using only numerals.

Example: Сейчас 9.10. – It's 9:10 a.m. now.

However, you should also know how to use the 'минута' – 'minute' word. Just like the 'час' word, it changes according to the numeral.

a) 1, 21 – Минута

b) 2, 3, 4, 22, 23, and 24 – Минуты

c) 5-20 – Минут

The same happens to the word 'секунда' – 'second', although telling the time using seconds is rarely necessary.

Example: Ways of saying 'It's 3:15 a.m. now':

Сейчас три пятнадцать.

Сейчас три пятнадцать утра.

Сейчас три часа пятнадцать минут.

As you see, the word 'утра' can be omitted, because the numerals make it clear.

RUSSIAN EQUIVALENTS FOR 'TO', 'PAST', 'HALF', AND 'QUARTER'

1) 'To' – 'Без' – Means that some minutes will pass before the hour. In general context, 'без' means 'without'.

Без двадцати два – Twenty minutes to two

The minutes should be in the genitive case. For your convenience, you can memorize the most common numerals Russians use in this expression.

One minute to two. – Без одной (минуты) два.
Five minutes to two. – Без пяти (минут) два.
Ten minutes to two. – Без десяти (минут) два.
Fifteen minutes to two. – Без пятнадцати (минут) два.
Twenty minutes to two. – Без двадцати (минут) два.

2) The situation with using **'past'** when talking about time is a bit more complicated as it's expressed through the case form and employs a different logic when compared to the English expression.

The Russian equivalent for **'Five minutes past six' is 'Пять минут седьмого'**, where 'седьмого' is the cardinal numeral of 'семь'.

Let's analyze the logic behind this expression. In the English version, the emphasis is on the fact that five minutes have passed since the short clock hand reached six. In Russian, the idea is that the long clock hand is already reaching out to the next hour, i.e., to seven in our case.

To form such expressions correctly, it's important to know cardinal numerals from 1 to 12 in the genitive case. To form the genitive case, simply replace the endings '-ый', '-ой', '-ий' with '-ого'.

ORDINAL NUMERALS 1-12

Cardinal	Ordinal (the nominative case)
Один	Первый
Два	Второй
Три	Третий
Четыре	Четвёртый
Пять	Пятый
Шесть	Шестой
Семь	Седьмой
Восемь	Восьмой
Девять	Девятый
Десять	Десятый
Одиннадцать	Одиннадцатый
Двенадцать	Двенадцатый

Example: Сейчас десять минут второго. – It's ten past one now.

3) The Russian words for **'half' and 'quarter'** are 'половина' and 'четверть'. The Russian equivalent for 'half past two' is 'половина третьего'. This expression uses the same logic as in the previous case.

The Russian equivalent for **'quarter to nine'** is **'без четверти девять'**. Note that the word 'четверть' changes its ending.

The Russian equivalent for **'quarter past nine'** is **'четверть десятого'**, again, with different logic for Russian and English.

Question	Sample Answers
Сколько (сейчас) времени? What time is it (now)?	**(Сейчас) Шесть десять.** It's ten past six (now). **Пять вечера.** It's five p.m. **Двенадцать часов.** It's twelve o'clock. **Двадцать минут четвёртого.** It's twenty past three.
Который час? What time is it?	**Без пятнадцати минут одиннадцать.** It's fifteen to eleven.
Вы не могли бы сказать, который час? **(Used for asking strangers)** Could you tell me the time, please?	**Да, конечно! Сейчас четверть десятого.** Yes, of course! It's a quarter past nine.
Скажите пожалуйста, сколько сейчас времени? (Can be used to ask strangers and people whom you would address with 'Вы'). Could you tell me what time is it now?	**Семь тридцать пять.** Seven thirty-five.
Во сколько ты приходишь на работу? At what time do you come to work?	**Я прихожу на работу ровно в восемь часов утра.** I come to work at 8 a.m. sharp.

 Pay special attention to the last example. The preposition 'в' is the Russian equivalent for 'at' when we say that something happens at a certain time.

🔊 HOBBIES AND PASTIMES VOCABULARY LIST

Russian	English
отдыхать/отдыхаю	have a rest
проводить/провожу свободное время	spend free time
активный/пассивный отдых	active/passive relaxation
оставаться/остаюсь дома	stay home
смотреть/смотрю фильмы, телевизор	watch movies, TV
детектив	detective
комедия	comedy
мелодрама	love story
триллер	thriller
фильм ужасов	horror film
сидеть/сижу в интернете	surf the net
готовить/готовлю	cook
плавать/плаваю ходить/хожу в бассейн	swim go to the swimming pool
рисование рисовать/рисую	painting paint/draw
чтение читать/читаю	reading read
танцы танцую/танцевать ходить/хожу на танцы	dancing dance go dancing

пение петь/пою	singing sing
заниматься/занимаюсь садом, огородом (noun in prepositional)	work in the garden, vegetable garden
заниматься/занимаюсь спортом (noun in prepositional)	do sports
играть/играю в футбол, баскетбол, шахматы	play football, basketball, chess
собирать/собираю марки, монеты…	collect stamps, coins…
кататься/катаюсь на велосипеде	ride a bike
ходить/хожу в походы	go hiking
путешествовать/путешествую	travel
ходить/хожу в кино, театр, музеи	go to the cinema, theatre, museums
ездить, ходить/езжу, хожу на экскурсии	go on excursions (the first word implies going by a vehicle)
иностранные языки изучать/изучаю языки	foreign languages study languages
заниматься/занимаюсь йогой (noun in prepositional)	do yoga
музыка слушать/слушаю музыку играть/играю на гитаре, барабане, скрипке, пианино	music listen to the music play the guitar, the drums, the violin, the piano
фотография фотографировать/фотографирую	photography take photos
встречаться/встречаюсь с друзьями	meet friends
интересоваться/интересуюсь + noun in prepositional	to be interested in
увлекаться/увлекаюсь + noun in prepositional	to be into, to be keen on

🔊 ASKING AND ANSWERING QUESTIONS ABOUT PASTIMES AND HOBBIES*

Question	Example Answer
У тебя есть хобби? Do you have a hobby?	**Да, у меня есть хобби.** Yes, I have a hobby. **Нет, у меня нет хобби.** No, I don't have a hobby.
Тебе нравится/ты любишь танцевать? Do you like dancing?	**Да (нет), мне (не) нравится/я (не) люблю танцевать.** Yes (no), I (don't) like dancing.
Что ты делаешь в свободное время? What do you do in your free time?	**В свободное время я встречаюсь с друзьями.** In my free time I meet my friends.
Что ты любишь делать? What do you like doing?	**Я люблю кататься на велосипеде.** I like riding a bike.
Чем ты любишь/тебе нравится заниматься? What do you like doing?	**Я люблю/мне нравится заниматься рисованием.** I like painting.
Чем ты увлекаешься? What are you keen on?	**Я увлекаюсь чтением.** I'm keen on reading.
Чем ты интересуешься? What are you interested in?	**Я интересуюсь фотографией.** I am into photography.
Что тебе нравится больше: рисование или плавание? What do you like more: painting or swimming?	**Мне больше нравится плавание.** I like swimming more.
Какая музыка тебе нравится? What kind of music do you like?	**Мне нравится рок-музыка.** I like rock music.
Какие фильмы тебе нравятся? What kind of movies do you like? **Какой твой любимый фильм?** What is your favorite movie?	**Мне нравятся комедии.** I like comedies. **Мой любимый фильм – «Достучаться до небес».** My favorite movie is 'Knocking on Heaven's Door'.

*Note that all questions are based on asking someone you can address with 'ты'.

POSSESSIVE PRONOUNS IN COMBINATION WITH NOUNS

When used with nouns, possessive pronouns correspond in gender, number, and case. The pronoun depends on the noun, i.e., its forms are defined by the noun.

See how to use possessive pronouns in the expressions you've learned before:

Name: Possessive pronoun in accusative + noun in accusative + зовут

Её сестру зовут Анжела. – Her sister's name is Angela.

Age: Possessive pronoun in dative + noun in dative + number + лет/года/год

Твоему сыну шесть лет. – Your son is six years old.

Possession: У + possessive pronoun in genitive + noun in genitive + есть + noun in accusative

У **моего** брата есть машина. – My brother has got a car.

Absence of possession: У + possessive pronoun in genitive + noun in genitive + нет + noun in genitive

У **нашего** сына нет свободного времени. – Our son doesn't have any free time.

Likes/dislikes: Possessive pronoun in dative + noun in dative + (не) нравится

Моей подруге (не) нравится петь. – My friend (dis)likes singing.

USEFUL EXPRESSIONS WITH NOUNS IN DIFFERENT CASES

The information below provides common situations when different cases can be used. Consult the Grammar Appendix to see how to use these case forms, page 185.

Genitive case

1) Indicating the possessor. In the English language possession is often indicated with the help of 's' and the preposition 'of'. Note that in Russian the possessor always follows the object they possess.

Compare:
Dad's car – **Папина** машина.

2) When you would use **'of'** in English.

Compare:
I've got plenty **of experience**. – У меня много **опыта**.

3) When you would use **'any'** or **'some'** in English as well as **'много'** and **'мало'** – 'a lot of' and 'little', 'few'.

Compare:
Give me some **water**, please. – Дай мне **воды**, пожалуйста.

Dative case

1) With the verbs **'звонить – call', 'помогать – help', 'показывать – show', 'давать – give'.**

Я звоню **папе**. – I'm calling my **dad**.

2) With the preposition **'к'**, when it indicates movement towards an object or a person.

Example: Я хожу в гости **к** бабушк**е** по выходным. – I go to visit my grandmother on weekends.

Accusative case

1) Indicating the **object of possession**.

I have a **dog**. – У меня есть **собака**.

2) After prepositions **'в' – 'in, into'** and **'на' – 'on, to'** to indicate motion towards an object.

I'm going **to work**. – Я иду **на работу**.

Instrumental case

1) When you would use **'by'**, **'with'**, or **'by means of'** in English.

Я режу мясо **ножом**. – I'm cutting meat **with a knife**.

2) With the preposition **'с' – 'with'**.

Я приду с друг**ом**. – I'll come **with a friend**.

3) The parts of the day, if they answer the question 'when'.

Утром – In the morning

Днём – In the afternoon

Вечером – In the evening

Ночью – At night

Я позвоню тебе **утром**. – I'll call you **in the morning**.

4) Indicating professions in the phrase **'работать – work as'**.

Мой муж работает водител**ем**. – My husband works as a driver.

5) 'стать' – 'to become'.

Я хочу стать врач**ом**. – I want to become a doctor.

Prepositional case

1) With the preposition 'o' – 'about'.

Мы говорим о **спорте**. – We are talking about sports.

2) With the prepositions 'на' – 'at' and 'в' – 'in' indicating a place.

Я сейчас **на** работе. – I'm **at** work now.

Она **в** машине. – She's **in** the car.

 Preposition **'o'** can change into **'об'** when it's followed by a vowel, and into **'обо'** when it's followed by a consonant cluster, which is done for more convenient pronunciation.

Example:

Я не хочу думать **об** этом! – I don't want to think **of** it!

Вы говорите **обо мне**? – Are you talking **about me**?

THE PRESENT TENSE IN RUSSIAN

In the vocabulary above you've come across lots of verbs in the present tense.

For example:

Я встаю – I get up

Я умываюсь – I wash

Я разговариваю – I talk

The present tense in Russian expresses both habitual and current actions and is also used to express universal truths.

For example:

Сейчас я читаю. – I'm reading now. (current action)

Обычно я читаю вечером. – I usually read in the evening. (habitual)

Солнце встаёт на востоке. – The sun rises in the east. (universal truth)

So, Russian present tense corresponds to several English present tenses - present simple, present continuous, and present perfect continuous.

 The verbs in the present tense change according to the person and number, which is expressed in the ending. Some widespread verbs have irregular patterns of conjugation, so make sure to consult the Grammar Appendix for both regular and irregular forms (pages 186-189).

Я чита**ю** книгу. – I read a book. (1st person singular)

Ты чита**ешь** книгу. – You read a book. (2nd person singular)

Мы чита**ем** книгу. – We read a book. (1st person plural)

REFLEXIVE VERBS IN RUSSIAN

Reflexive verbs correspond to the concept of '-self' in English. You've already come across them in the vocabulary section.

Example:

Умываться – wash

Я умываюсь – I wash

With reflexive verbs the subject and the object of the sentence are the same. In 'Я одеваюсь – I get dressed' we see that 'Я' performs the action and is simultaneously the object to which the action is directed.

 To conjugate the verbs that end in postfixes **'-ся'** or **'-сь'**, just remove the postfixes, perform the conjugation, and put them back in place.

Example:

Просыпаться (wake up) – просыпать – просыпаю – просыпаюсь

Compare:

Я одеваюсь

I get dressed

Я одеваю свою дочь

I'm dressing my daughter

THE REFLEXIVE PRONOUN 'СЕБЯ'

'Себя' is used to imply '-self' when the use of the reflexive verb is not possible. These pronouns always refer to the same object as the subject of the sentence.

Example:

Она рассказывает **о себе**. – She's talking about herself.

Он разговаривает **с собой**. – He's talking to himself.

Она купила **себе** новое платье. – She bought herself a new dress.

 Note two important things:

- 'Себя' changes according to case like the pronoun 'ты': 'тебя – себя, тебе – себе, тобой – собой'.
- 'Себя' is never to be used in combination with a reflexive verb.

TIME EXPRESSIONS WITH PREPOSITIONS AND CASES

Ways to express duration

1) Accusative case of the time period expresses how long the action lasts/lasted.

Я работаю в саду **полчаса** каждый день. – I work in the garden **for half an hour** every day.

Я еду на работу **два часа**. – I drive to work **for two hours**.

Она провела в отпуске **неделю**. – She spent **a week** on vacation.

Они не были дома **пять месяцев**. – They haven't been home **for five months**.

2) На + accusative case of the time period that will take place after the action of the verb is finished.

Я еду к родителям **на неделю**. – I'm going to my parents' **for a week**.

(It means that after I arrive at my parents' I will spend a week there).

Он ушёл погулять **на два часа**. – He left for a walk **for two hours**.

(After he leaves, he will spend two hours walking).

3) Через + accusative case indicates the time period after which the action will start.

Я буду готова **через** минуту. – I'll be ready **in a minute**.

Мы приедем **через** неделю. – We'll come **in a week**.

Ways to express frequency

1) Каждый (every) + time period in the accusative case.

Я хожу в бассейн **каждую** среду. – I go to the swimming **pool every Wednesday**.
Мы звоним родителям **каждый** день. – We call our parents **every day**.

2) По + dative plural to indicate habitually repeated actions.

Они гуляют **по вечерам**. – They go for a walk **in the evenings**.
Вы смотрите фильмы **по пятницам**. – You watch movies **on Fridays**.

3) Раз в + accusative.

Она занимается йогой **три раза в неделю**. – She does yoga **three times a week**.
У меня отпуск **два раза в год**. – I have a holiday **twice a year**.

Ways to express a certain time
(non-punctual time)

1) Time periods shorter than a week – в + accusative case.

Вы позвоните мне **в понедельник**? – Will you call me **on Monday**?
Она засыпает **в одиннадцать часов**. – She falls asleep **at eleven o'clock**.

2) With the word 'неделя - week' – на + prepositional case.

Давай встретимся **на этой неделе**. – Let's meet **this week**.
Я буду свободна на **следующей неделе**. – I'll be free **next week**.

3) Time periods longer than a week – в + prepositional case.

Я получу повышение **в ноябре**. – I'll get a promotion **in November**.
Мы заканчиваем школу **в этом году**. – We're finishing school **this year**.

Exceptions:

Seasons (зима – winter, весна – spring, лето – summer, осень – autumn) and **parts of the day** (утро – morning, день – day, вечер – evening, ночь – night) are to be in the instrumental case without any prepositions.

Я вернусь **осенью**. – I'll come back **in autumn**.
Он перезвонит **вечером**. – He'll call back **in the evening**.

4) By a certain time in the future – к + dative case.

Доклад мне нужен **к пятнице**. – I need the report **by Friday**.
Она будет готова **к пяти часам**. – She'll be ready **by five o'clock**.

Ways to express a certain time
(punctual time)

1) When more than one time period is combined (hour, day, month, year) – genitive case without any prepositions.

Она родилась **второго мая тысяча девятьсот восемьдесят шестого года**. – She was born on **May 2, 1986**.

Мы придём в **два часа дня**. – We'll come **at 2 o'clock in the afternoon (2 p.m.)**.

2) Approximate punctual time – около + genitive case or reverse the order of the noun and the number with the preposition 'в' in the middle.

Мы заберём детей **около восьми часов**. – We'll pick up the kids **at about 8 o'clock**.

Я приду **часов в семь**. – I'll come **at about 7 o'clock**.

📝 EXERCISES

01. Match the actions with the images.

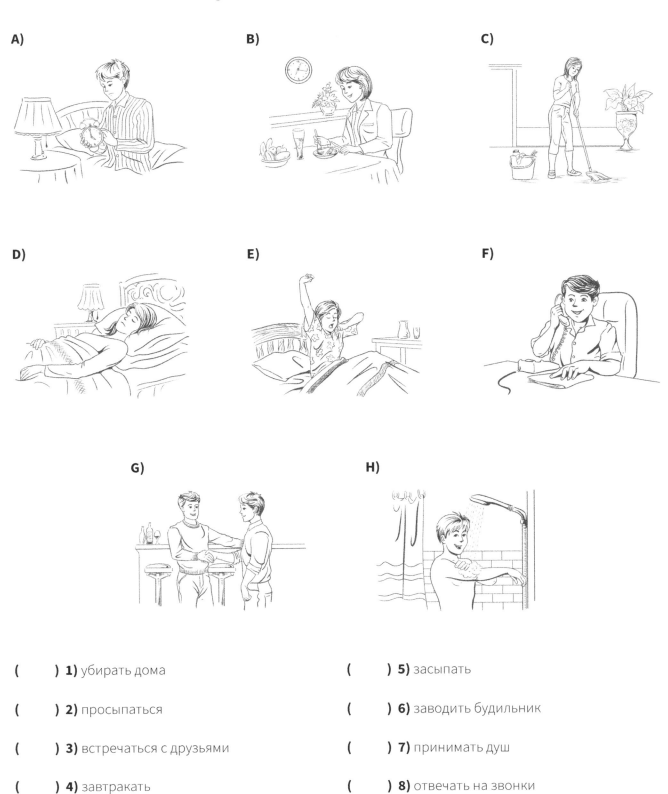

A)

B)

C)

D)

E)

F)

G)

H)

(   ) **1)** убирать дома

(   ) **2)** просыпаться

(   ) **3)** встречаться с друзьями

(   ) **4)** завтракать

(   ) **5)** засыпать

(   ) **6)** заводить будильник

(   ) **7)** принимать душ

(   ) **8)** отвечать на звонки

02. What case of noun would you use to express possession? Check the appendix and make sentences according to the sample.

Sample: Друг/сестра – Друг сестр**ы** – Sister's friend.

1) Дом/родители _____.

2) Начальник/коллега _____.

3) Деньги/муж _____.

4) Машина/племянница _____.

5) Книги/студенты _____.

6) Братья/друг _____.

7) Учитель/дети _____.

8) Жена/брат _____.

03. Expand the above word combinations into sentences. Use the genitive case of the corresponding possessive pronouns.

Sample: Друг/я/сестра – Это друг мо**ей** сестр**ы** – This is my sister's friend.

1) Дом/ты/родители _____.

2) Начальник/они/коллега _____.

3) Деньги/она/муж _____.

4) Машина/он/племянница _____.

5) Книги/мы/студенты _____.

6) Братья/мой/друг _____.

7) Учитель/вы/дети _____.

8) Жена/я/брат _____.

04. Complete these sentences with nouns in genitive.

1) Утром у меня очень мало (время). Я часто опаздываю на работу. _____.

I have very little time in the morning. I'm often late for work.

2) Сегодня я дома одна, без (дети). _____.

I'm home alone today, without the kids.

3) У меня нет (братья) или (сёстры). Я единственный ребёнок в семье. _____.

I don't have any brothers or sisters. I'm an only child in the family.

4) В нашей больнице мало (врач). _____.

There are few doctors in our hospital.

5) Интересно, почему (начальник) нет сегодня в офисе? _____.

I wonder why the boss is not in the office today?

6) Я хочу много (деньги) и я много работаю. _____.

I want to have much money and I work a lot.

7) Здесь так жарко! Дайте мне (вода), пожалуйста. _____.

It's so hot here! Give me some water, please.

8) Здесь так мало (люди)! Почему? _____.

There are so few people here! Why?

9) Девочки, давайте пойдём в кафе без (мужья)! _____.

Girls, let's go to the café without our husbands!

10) После работы мне нужно немного (отдых). _____.

I need some rest after work.

05. Read these conversations and fill in the right form of negation 'нет', 'не', or 'ни'. Pay attention to the useful phrases in bold and see their translation in the English version. Then check your work with the audio and roleplay or read.

Conversation I

A: У тебя есть хобби?

B: _____, у меня нет хобби.

A: Ты шутишь? Тебе ничего _____ нравится?

B: Ну, мне нравится танцевать, но это _____ моё хобби. **Более того**, у меня почти _____ свободного времени!

A: Я тебя понимаю! Я тоже всегда занят!

Conversation I – English

A: Do you have a hobby?

B: No, I don't have a hobby.

A: Are you kidding? Don't you like anything?

B: Well, I like dancing but it's not my hobby. **Moreover**, I have almost no spare time.

A: I understand you! I'm always busy too!

Conversation II

A: Как ты добираешься до университета?

B: Я хожу пешком.

A: Пешком? **У тебя что,** _____ денег на автобус или метро?

B: _____, у меня есть деньги! **Просто** мой университет _____ далеко. Дорога занимает у меня десять минут.

A: О, ты **счастливчик**! Я никогда _____ хожу в университет пешком.

Conversation II - English

A: How do you get to the university?

B: I go on foot.

A: On foot? **Don't you have** money for a bus or the subway?

B: Yes I do, I have money! **It's just because** my university is not far away. It takes me ten minutes to get there.

A: Oh, you're **a lucky guy**! I never go to the university on foot!

Conversation III

A: Извините, Виктор Иванович здесь?

B: _____, его _____. Он на совещании.

A: Он скоро закончит?

B: Нет, _____ скоро. Хотите подождать?

A: _____, спасибо! Я зайду завтра.

Conversation III – English

A: Excuse me, is Victor Ivanovich here?

B: No, he is not here. He's at a meeting.

A: Will he finish soon?

B: No, he won't. Would you like to wait?

A: No, thank you! I'll come tomorrow.

Conversation IV

A: Ты увлекаешься плаванием или рисованием?

B: Я не увлекаюсь _____ плаванием, _____ рисованием.

A: Правда? Мне казалось, ты хочешь стать художником.

B: _____, я _____ хочу стать художником. Я ещё _____ решила.

A: Но тебе уже шестнадцать. **Пора** решать!

B: Никогда _____ **поздно**! Я решу!

Conversation IV – English

A: Are you into swimming or painting?

B: I'm neither into swimming nor painting.

A: Really? **It seemed to me** you wanted to become a painter.

B: No, I don't want to become a painter. I haven't made up my mind yet.

A: But you're sixteen already! **It's time** to make up your mind!

B: It's never too late. I'll make up my mind!

Conversation V

A: У тебя есть минутка?

B: Вообще-то, _____. Я очень спешу. **Что случилось?**

A: Ты говоришь по-немецки?

B: Да, немного. **А что такое?**

A: Я _____ понимаю эту инструкцию. Можешь помочь мне сейчас?

B: Извини, _____ сейчас. Я опаздываю на работу. Сейчас у меня _____ времени.

A: Ладно. Я попробую онлайн-переводчик.

B: Ты _____ злишься? Я и правда очень спешу!

A: Конечно _____! **Я всё понимаю**!

Conversation V – English

A: Do you have a spare minute?

B: I don't, actually. I'm in a great hurry. What's up?

A: Do you speak German?

B: Yes, a bit. **Why?**

A: I don't understand this manual. Can you help me now?

B: Sorry, not now. I'm running late for work. I don't have any time now.

A: Okay, I'll try an online translating tool.

B: You're not angry, are you? I'm really in a great hurry!

A: Of course not! **I totally understand!**

06. Answer these questions with negation. Remember that absence of possession requires the genitive case of nouns and pronouns. Note that in some questions you'll be addressed in a formal way.

1) У тебя есть сестра?

_____.

2) Вы говорите по-испански?

_____.

3) Ты замужем/женат?

_____.

4) У Вас есть дети?

_____.

5) Тебе нравится играть в футбол?

_____.

6) У тебя есть машина?

_____.

7) Вам нравится Ваша работа?

_____.

8) У тебя много свободного времени вечером?

_____.

9) Ваш рабочий день начинается в семь утра?

_____.

10) Твои дети добираются до школы на автобусе?

_____.

_____.

07. Match the actions with the images.

A)

B)

C)

D)

E)

F)

G)

H)

(   ) **1)** собирать марки

(   ) **2)** играть на барабанах

(   ) **3)** танцевать

(   ) **4)** играть в шахматы

(   ) **5)** ходить в театр

(   ) **6)** интересоваться историей

(   ) **7)** слушать музыку

(   ) **8)** кататься на велосипеде

08. Complete these sentences with nouns and pronouns in the dative case.

1) По утрам я помогаю (жена) одевать детей. _____.

In the morning I help my wife to dress the kids.

2) (Мои родители) не нравится мой парень. _____.

My parents don't like my boyfriend.

3) Я часто звоню (друзья) после работы. _____.

I often call my friends after work.

4) (Моя подруга) очень нравятся триллеры. _____.

My friend likes thrillers a lot.

5) (Твоя дочь) нравятся эти очки? _____.

Does your daughter like these glasses?

6) На выходных я иногда хожу в гости к (мама). _____.

On weekends I sometimes go to visit my mom.

7) Я даю (дети) готовый обед в школу. _____.

I give my kids a ready-made lunch for their school.

8) (Мой муж) не нравится активный отдых. _____.

My husband doesn't like active relaxation.

9) Я всегда помогаю (коллеги) на работе. _____.

I always help my colleagues at work.

10) (Твоя сестра) нравится её новая работа? _____.

Does your sister like her new job?

11) Хороший отдых даёт (люди) много энергии. _____.

Good rest gives people lots of energy.

12) (Его брат) не нравится рок-музыка. _____.

His brother doesn't like rock music.

09. Make sentences about likes/dislikes using the information in the images. A check mark goes for 'нравится' and a cross goes for 'не нравится'. If needed, go back to the vocabulary section to find the words for depicted activities.

Also note that you'll need the dative case of Russian proper names (they are declined just like regular nouns depending on their gender and number). Write down the sentences in the lines next to the images and check the translations in the answer key.

Sample: (Сергей) не нравится опаздывать на работу. – Sergey doesn't like being late for work.

(✔) 1) _____

_____ .

(**X**) 2) _____

_____ .

(✔) 3) _____

_____ .

(✔) 4) _____

_____ .

(X) 5) _____

_____ .

(✔) 6) _____

_____ .

(X) 7) _____

_____ .

(**X**) 8) _____

_____ .

(**✓**) 9) _____

_____ .

(**✓**) 10) _____

_____ .

10. Make the sentences from the previous exercises true for yourself, your friend, child, or relative. Use nouns instead of names.

Example: Моему мужу не нравится опаздывать на работу. – My husband doesn't like being late for work.

1) _____

_____.

2) _____

_____.

3) _____

_____.

4) _____

_____.

5) _____

_____.

6) _____

_____.

7) _____

_____.

8) _____

_____.

9) _____

_____.

10) _____

_____.

11. Complete these sentences with nouns and pronouns in the accusative case.

1) Я не хожу на (работа) по понедельникам. _____.
I don't go to work on Mondays.

2) Я хорошо знаю (твоя сестра). _____.
I know your sister well.

3) Она слушает только классическую (музыка). _____.
She listens only to classical music.

4) Я редко готовлю (завтрак). _____.
I rarely cook breakfast.

5) У его сына есть (мотоцикл). _____.
His son has a motorcycle.

6) Я не понимаю (твой друг). Он говорит по-русски? _____.
I don't understand your friend. Does he speak Russian?

7) Давай пригласим твою (тётя) на чай. _____.
Let's invite your aunt for tea.

8) Я никогда не хожу в (наша столовая). _____.
I never go to our cafeteria.

9) Они не помнят (моя подруга). _____.
They don't remember my friend.

10) Я всегда укладываю (дети) рано. _____.
I always put kids to sleep early.

11) Она редко читает (книги) перед сном. _____.
She rarely reads books before going to bed.

12) Я вижу (её муж) на работе каждый день. _____.
I see her husband at work every day.

13) Обычно я отвожу детей в (школа). _____.
Usually, it's me who takes the kids to school.

14) Мы не любим готовить (еда). _____.
We don't like cooking.

12. Fill in the texts with the nouns and pronouns from the box and put these words in the form of the accusative case. Listen to the texts to check your work and repeat after the speaker. If needed, consult the English translation below.

Text 1

> еда я моя обувь душ Бобик своя собака люди игрушки

Привет! Меня зовут Аня, и я обожаю **1)** _____. Его зовут Бобик, и он очень активный. Каждый день он

будит **2)** _____ без пятнадцати семь. Как будильник! Я принимаю **3)** _____ и готовлю **4)** _____

для Бобика. Да, он первый, потом я. Затем я одеваюсь и выгуливаю **5)** _____. Он очень дружелюбный

и обожает новых **6)** _____. У него есть **7)** _____, но Бобик часто выбирает мою **8)** _____!

Hi! My name is Anya and I love my dog. His name is Bobik and he's very active. Every day he wakes me up at a quarter to seven. Like an alarm clock! I take a shower and cook food for Bobik. Yes, he's first and me next. Then I get dressed and walk Bobik. He's very friendly and loves new people. He's got toys, but Bobik often chooses my shoes!

Text 2

> курсы свой начальник работа моя идея работа я
> мои коллеги своя работа

Я не люблю **1)** _____. Каждый день я встаю в шесть утра. Я еду на **2)** _____ на автобусе, потом

на метро и потом опять на автобусе. Мой начальник просто ненавидит **3)** _____! А я ненавижу

4) _____! Мне нравятся **5)** _____, но моя зарплата очень низкая! Я хожу на **6)** _____

программистов и хочу поменять **7)** _____. Моя семья поддерживает **8)** _____.

I don't like my job. Every day I wake up at six o'clock in the morning. I go to work by bus, then by the subway and then by bus again. My boss just hates me! And I hate my boss! I like my colleagues but my salary is very low! I attend a programming course and want to change my job. My family supports my idea.

Text 3

> свои друзья будильник фильмы еда пижама
> университет музыка

По выходным я обычно просыпаюсь в одиннадцать часов. Я не завожу **1)** _____. Я не снимаю

2) _____ до обеда. На выходных я не готовлю. Я заказываю **3)** _____. Иногда я приглашаю

4) _____. Мы слушаем **5)** _____, смотрим **6)** _____ и просто болтаем. В понедельник мы снова

пойдём в **7)** _____, так что нам нужен хороший отдых!

On weekends I usually wake up at eleven o'clock. I don't set the alarm clock. I don't take my pajamas off until lunch. I don't cook on weekends. I order food. Sometimes I invite my friends. We listen to music, watch movies, and just chat. On Monday we'll go to university again, so we need good rest!

13. Complete these sentences with nouns and pronouns in the instrumental case.

1) Я позвоню тебе (вечер). Хорошо? _____.
I'll call you in the evening. Okay?

2) Твоя жена работает (медсестра)? _____.
Does your wife work as a nurse?

3) Сегодня я занята (уборка). _____.
I'm busy cleaning the house today.

4) Ты интересуешься (политика)? _____.
Are you interested in politics?

5) Моя дочь мечтает стать (пилот). _____.
My daughter dreams of becoming a pilot.

6) В этом отеле можно останавливаться с (собаки). _____.
You can stay at this hotel with dogs.

7) Завтра (утро) я встаю очень рано. _____.
I get up very early tomorrow morning.

8) Она так гордится (своя дочь)! _____.
She's so proud of her daughter!

9) Сын моей подруги увлекается (балет). _____.
My friend's son is keen on ballet.

10) Я не люблю заниматься (спорт). _____.
I don't like doing sports.

11) Я не могу открыть дверь (твой ключ). _____.
I can't open the door with your key.

12) Я провожу выходные с (друзья). _____.
I spend weekends with my friends.

14. The sentences below say what people dream of becoming or what they work as. Your task is to identify the profession by an image, place the name of the profession in the instrumental case and create the correct subject form in the sentence. See the sample.

Sample: Дочь (моя подруга) хочет стать врачом. – **Дочь моей подруги** хочет стать врач**ом**.
My friend's daughter wants to become a doctor.

1) Сын (мои друзья) хочет стать

_____

_____ .

2) Муж (моя дочь) работает

_____

_____ .

3) Сосед (твой сын) мечтает стать

_____

_____ .

4) Коллега (его жена) мечтает стать

_____

_____ .

5) Жена (мой друг) работает

_____

_____ .

6) Дочь (ваш друг) работает

_____

_____ .

7) Сестра (твой муж) хочет стать

_____

_____ .

8) Друг (мой племянник) работает

_____

_____ .

15. Four people were asked about their interests. Complete their answers with the nouns in the instrumental case. Check your work with the audio.

I

A: Света, чем ты увлекаешься?
B: Я увлекаюсь (танцы). _____.

II

A: Макар, чем ты интересуешься?
B: Я интересуюсь (история). _____.

III

A: Матвей, чем ты занимаешься по выходным?
B: По выходным я занимаюсь (сад). _____.

IV

A: Алла, чем ты интересуешься?
B: Я интересуюсь иностранными (языки). _____.

16. Make sentences about yourself using the table below. What do you do in the morning, during the day, in the evening, and at night? There is no correct or wrong answer, just practice using parts of the day and daily routines vocabulary.

Sample: Утром я чищу зубы. – In the morning I brush my teeth.

Утром		Я	Просыпаюсь
			Просматриваю почту
			Умываюсь
			Ужинаю
Днем			Отвечаю на звонки
			Занимаюсь спортом
			Выгуливаю собаку
			Хожу на совещания
			Обедаю
Вечером			Делаю уборку
			Встречаюсь с друзьями
			Завтракаю
			Разговариваю по телефону
Ночью			Ложусь спать
			Хожу на прогулку
			Делаю зарядку

17. Complete these conversations with nouns and pronouns in the prepositional case. Check your work with the audio, consult the English translations when necessary, and roleplay or read the conversations. Also, pay attention to the useful expressions.

Conversation I

A: Что у тебя на (лицо) _____? Грязь?

B: Ой, да! Я работаю в (сад) _____ каждый вечер.

A: О, точно! Жена рассказывала мне о (твой сад) _____. **Ты молодец!**

B: Спасибо! У меня много стресса на (работа) _____. Сад помогает мне расслабиться.
A: Как я тебя понимаю!

Conversation I – English

A: What is it on your face? Dirt?
B: Oh, yes! I work in the garden every evening.
A: Oh, right! My wife told me about your garden. **Good for you!**
B: Thanks! I've got a lot of stress at work. The garden helps me relax.
A: I totally understand!

Conversation II

A: О чём ты думаешь, **дорогая**?

B: О (наше путешествие) _____. Сегодня я (дом) _____ и хочу всё спланировать.
A: Не волнуйся! Всё будет хорошо!

B: Надеюсь. Сейчас я думаю о (дети) _____. Они будут скучать по нам!

A: О, да ладно! Они не думают о (мы), они думают о (подарки) _____.
B: Точно! Нужно купить подарки детям!

A: И не забудь о (наши друзья) _____ и (твои родители) _____.

B: Спасибо, **дорогой**! В прошлый раз мы покупали подарки в (аэропорт)_____. Это было ужасно!

Conversation II – English

A: What are you thinking about, **darling**?
B: About our trip. I'm home today and want to plan everything.
A: Don't worry! Everything will be fine!
B: I hope so. I'm thinking about the kids now. Will they miss us?
A: Oh, come on! They don't think about us, they think about the presents!
B: Exactly! We need to buy presents for the kids!
A: And don't forget about our friends and your parents!
B: Thank you **darling! Last time we bought presents at the airport. That was horrible!

Conversation III

A: Андрей Иванович, я хочу поговорить с Вами.
B: Да, Алла Викторовна. О чём?

A: О (Ваша пенсия) _____.

B: О (моя пенсия) _____? **А что не так**?

A: Всё так! Я просто думала о небольшой (вечеринка) _____.
B: О, нет!
A: Но почему? Вы всегда думаете о (люди) _____. Сегодня люди хотят сказать Вам спасибо!
B: Сегодня? Вечеринка сегодня?

A: Вообще-то, да! Вечеринка в (офис) _____!

Conversation III – English

A: Andrey Ivanovich, I'd like to talk to you.

B: Yes, Alla Victorovna. What is it about?

A: About your retirement.

B: About my retirement? **What is wrong**?

A: Nothing is wrong! I was just thinking of a little party.

B: Oh, no!

A: But why? You always care about people. Today people want to thank you!

B: Today? The party is today?

A: Actually, yes! A party at the office!

18. Complete these sentences using the right forms of the verbs in brackets.

1) Моя жена (гулять) с собакой по утрам, а я – по вечерам. _____ .
My wife walks the dog in the mornings and I do it in the evenings.

2) Мои соседи (хотеть) купить новую машину. _____
My neighbors want to buy a new car.

3) Мы с мужем (смотреть) сериалы по субботам. _____
My husband and I watch series on Saturdays.

4) Ваша дочь каждый день (опаздывать) в школу. _____ .
Your daughter is late for school every day.

5) Как ты (добираться) до работы? _____ .
How do you get to work?

6) Наши дети слишком много (сидеть) в интернете! _____ .
Our kids surf the net too much!

7) Сын моей подруги (играть) в футбол каждый четверг. _____ .
My friend's son plays football every Thursday.

8) Чем Вы (увлекаться)? _____ .
What are you keen on?

9) Во сколько твой муж (просыпаться) по будням? _____ .
At what time does your husband wake up on weekdays?

10) Почему ты (ненавидеть) йогу? _____ .
Why do you hate yoga?

11) Моя коллега очень хорошо (рисовать). _____
My colleague paints very well.

12) Мой муж (бриться) каждое утро. _____ .
My husband shaves every morning.

13) Я никогда не (засыпать) до полуночи. _____ .
I never fall asleep before midnight.

14) Обычно мой муж (забирать) детей из садика. _____ .
Usually, my husband picks up the kids from kindergarten.

19. As you know, the verb 'хотеть – want' is conjugated according to an irregular pattern. While it's not the only verb that does this, it's a very widespread verb. So, let's pay more attention to it.

Use the right form of the verb 'хотеть' for the subject in the first column, listen and match the columns to find out what people/animals want and put down the whole sentence. Remember to consult the answer key. The first is done for you.

1 – E. Моя собака **хочет** гулять утром, днём и вечером.

Subject	Wish
1) моя собака	**A)** приготовить вкусный ужин
2) твои друзья	**B)** заниматься танцами
3) мы с дочерью	**C)** ходить в кино по субботам
4) ты	**D)** поменять работу
5) её сын	**E)** гулять утром, днём и вечером
6) ты и твой брат	**F)** купить новую игрушку
7) я	**G)** играть в компьютерные игры
8) ваша племянница	**H)** спать весь день
9) наши коллеги	**I)** возвращаться домой рано
10) их начальник	**J)** добираться до работы на машине
11) ваши дети	**K)** проводить выходные вместе
12) мой сосед	**L)** засыпать рано
13) его кот	**M)** читать на русском языке

(   ) 1) _____ .

(   ) 2) _____ .

(   ) 3) _____ .

(   ) 4) _____ .

(   ) 5) _____ .

(   ) 6) _____ .

(   ) 7) _____ .

(   ) 8) _____ .

(   ) 9) _____ .

(   ) 10) _____ .

(   ) 11) _____ .

(   ) 12) _____ .

(   ) 13) _____ .

20. Go back to exercise 15 and replace 'я' with 'ты, мы, вы, он, она, они' and change the verbs accordingly. While there is no right answer in terms of what actions people perform during different parts of the day, there are correct answers for the forms of the verbs, so check them in the answer key.

21. Tell the time on these clocks and write down what Nikita does at this or that time of the day.

Sample: В пятнадцать минут второго Никита обедает. – At a quarter past one Nikita has lunch.

Note that there may be several correct ways to tell the time, so there will be several answers in the answer key. Try to provide several ways of telling the time too.

1) _____

_____.

2) _____

_____.

3) _____

_____.

4) _____

_____.

5) _____

_____.

6) _____

_____.

7) _____

_____ .

8) _____

_____ .

9) _____

_____ .

10) _____

_____ .

11) _____

_____ .

12) _____

_____ .

22. Go back to exercise 19 and tell us what you usually do at this time of the day.

23. Listen to the text about Masha and her friends Sergey and Andrey. Place a check mark in the columns to state the frequency of the actions they perform. Then write down the sentences according to the table and see the answer key for the text and its English translation. Listen to the text again and repeat after the speaker.

	Маша				
	Ходить в бассейн	Бегать по утрам	Работать из дома	Ложиться спать рано	Ходить в спортзал
Часто					
Редко					
Всегда					
Никогда не					
Обычно					
Иногда					
Каждый день					
Раз в неделю					
По вторникам					
По средам					

	Сергей и Андрей				
	Ходить в бассейн	Бегать по утрам	Работать из дома	Ложиться спать рано	Ходить в спортзал
Часто					
Редко					
Всегда					
Никогда не					
Обычно					
Иногда					
Каждый день					
Раз в неделю					
По вторникам					
По средам					

24. Go back to exercise 21 and ask your partner how often they perform these actions, then ask your partner to do the same for you. If you don't have a partner, imagine asking your friend. Note that the verb forms for the 2nd person singular and the 1st person singular are in the answer key.

Sample: Как часто ты ходишь в бассейн? – Я хожу в бассейн три раза в неделю.
How often do you go to the swimming pool? – I go to the swimming pool three times a week.

25. Complete these conversations by filling in the correct prepositions and roleplay the dialogues after checking your work. As usual, pay attention to useful expressions in bold.

Conversation I

A: Что ты делаешь **1)** _____пятницу?

B: Ничего особенного. А что?

A: 2) _____неделю я заканчиваю свой проект на работе и хочу отметить это.

B: Звучит здорово! 3) _____пятницам я обычно навещаю маму, но я могу изменить свои планы.

A: Здорово! Тогда жду тебя **4)** _____пятницу, **5)** _____половину седьмого **у** меня дома.

A: What are you doing on Friday?
B: Nothing special. Why?
A: In a week I'll finish my project at work and want to celebrate it.
B: Sounds great! On Fridays I usually visit my mom, but I can change my plans.
A: Great! Then I'll be waiting for you on Friday at half past six **at my place.**

Conversation II

A: 1) _____четверг я еду к родителям **2)** _____неделю.

B: Опять? Ты ездишь к родителям **3)** _____месяц!

A: Ну и что? 4) _____три дня у мамы **день рождения**. Я хочу быть с ней.

B: Но **5)** _____вторникам мы ужинаем у моих родителей!

A: Я помню, но это день рождения! Давай навестим твоих родителей **6)** _____следующей неделе?

B: Ладно, договорились!

A: On Thursday I'm going to my parents' for a week.
B: Again? You go to your parents' every month!
A: So what? It's my mom's **birthday** in three days. I want to be with her.
B: But on Tuesdays we have dinner at my parents'.
A: I remember, but it's a birthday! Let's visit your parents next week!
B: Okay, deal!

Conversation III

A: Дорогие коллеги, у меня есть новость! Начальник хочет закончить проект **1)** _____ понедельнику.

B: О, нет! **Это невозможно! 2)** _____ среде, да! Но не понедельник!

A: Я понимаю. **Это сложно**. Но это только раз **3)** _____ год. Обычно мы не спешим.

C: Раз в год? А **4)** _____ прошлой неделе? Мы закончили **5)** _____ девяти часов вечера!

A: Хорошо, как насчёт вторника? Мы закончим **6)** _____ вторнику?

B: Может быть, может быть …

A: Dear colleagues, I've got news. The boss wants to finish the project by Monday.
B: Oh, no! **It's impossible!** By Wednesday, yes! But not Monday!
A: I understand. **It's hard**. But it's only once a year. We're not in a hurry usually.
C: Once a year? And last week? We finished at about nine p.m.!
A: Okay, what about Tuesday? Will we finish by Tuesday?
B: Maybe, maybe …

UNIT III
TRAVELING AND NAVIGATION

This unit features vocabulary and grammar constructions you'll need when travelling as well as for expressing movement-related actions both during a trip and in your everyday life.

Vocabulary

To start building your vocabulary, read and listen to this text, then compare it with the English translation paragraph by paragraph.

🔊 Мой родной город – My native town

Привет, меня зовут Артём. Это мой родной город. Он **привлекает** много туристов. В городе есть исторический музей и много **памятников**.

Hi, my name is Artyom. This is my hometown. It **attracts** many tourists. There is a historical museum in the town, and many **monuments**.

Гости нашего города часто **ходят на экскурсии**. Я тоже приглашаю вас на экскурсию. Поехали! Итак, люди **приезжают в** наш город **на поездах, автобусах или машинах**. Это **небольшой** город, так что у нас нет **аэропорта**. У нас есть **несколько гостиниц** и **два хостела**. Сначала туристы **заселяются**, а потом идут **осматривать достопримечательности**.

The visitors to our town often **go on tours**. I invite you on a tour as well. Let's go! So, people **come to** our town **by train**, **bus or car**. It's **not a big** city, so there is no **airport**. We've got **a few hotels** and **two hostels**. First, tourists **check in** and then go **to see the sights**.

Вы можете **повернуть налево, направо** или **пойти прямо** – история **везде**! Можно **поехать на такси**, **на автобусе, на трамвае, троллейбусе** или **на маршрутке**. Что такое маршрутка? Это микроавтобус, который ходит по тому же маршруту, что и обычный городской автобус, он более комфортный и едет быстрее. **Заходите в** большие и маленькие музеи, посещайте наши **выставки** и наслаждайтесь!

You can **turn left** or **right** or **go straight ahead** – history **is everywhere**! You can **go by taxi**, **by bus**, **by streetcar**, **by trolleybus** or **by marshrutka**. What is marshrutka? It's a minibus that runs along the same route as the usual city bus, but it's more comfortable and goes at a higher speed. **Drop by** our big and small museums, visit our **exhibitions** and enjoy!

Мой город, конечно, исторический, но он и **современный** тоже! У нас есть **ночные клубы**, дискотеки, а также много спортивных клубов. Например, **вот в этом здании находится** клуб фотографов. Вам понравилась моя экскурсия? Что бы вы хотели посетить?

Of course, my town is a historic one, but it's **modern** too! We've got **night clubs**, discos as well as many sports clubs. For example, **there is** a photography club **in this building**. Did you like my tour? What would you like to visit?

🔊 PLACES AND OBJECTS IN THE CITY

аэропорт	airport
вокзал	railway station
автостанция	bus station
метро/станция метро	subway/subway station
остановка	bus station (can be used for other means of public transport as well: streetcar/metro/bus etc.)
гостиница	hotel
магазин	shop
супермаркет	supermarket
торговый центр	mall
универмаг	department store
рынок	market
кафе	café
ресторан	restaurant
бар	bar
почта	post office
библиотека	library
школа	school
банк	bank
церковь	church
собор	cathedral

больница	hospital
аптека	drug store
полиция	police station
парк	park
кинотеатр	cinema
театр	theater
памятник	monument
туалет	restroom, toilet
перекрёсток	crossroads
улица	street
проспект	avenue
переулок	alley
площадь	square
пешеходный переход	pedestrian crossing
светофор	traffic lights
подземный переход	underpass
поворот	turn
район	district
парковка	parking lot
заправка	gas station
здание	building

🔊 ACTIONS AND VERBS OF MOVEMENT

приезжать в + accusative case	to come to (by vehicle)
прибывать в/на + accusative case	to arrive at
ввернуться из + genitive case вернуться домой	to return from to go back home
ехать/приехать на + transport in the prepositional case	to go/come or arrive by + means of transport
уехать из + genitive	to leave
лететь/прилететь на самолёте (prepositional)	to fly/arrive by plane
сойти с самолёта (genitive)	to get off the plane
садиться в (транспорт) + accusative	to get on/into (transport)
входить в + accusative	to enter
выходить из + genitive	to get off/out of
спросить дорогу	to ask directions
спросить у + genitive	to ask somebody
брать/вызывать такси	to take/call a taxi
бронировать (заранее)	to book (in advance)
заселяться/выселяться	to check in/out
осматривать достопримечательности	to see the sights
фотографировать	to take photos
идти/ходить* в/на + place in the accusative case	to go to
бегать/бежать* в/на + place in the accusative case	to run to
ехать/ездить* в + place in the accusative case ехать/ездить* на + vehicle in the prepositional case	to go (by vehicle) to/by to go (by vehicle) by
посещать	to visit
наслаждаться	to enjoy
переходить дорогу	to cross the road
повернуть налево/направо	to turn left/right
идти прямо	to go straight ahead
дойти до + genitive	to get to
свернуть на + accusative	to turn to
покупать	to buy
платить за/оплачивать	to pay for

🔊 MEANS OF TRANSPORT

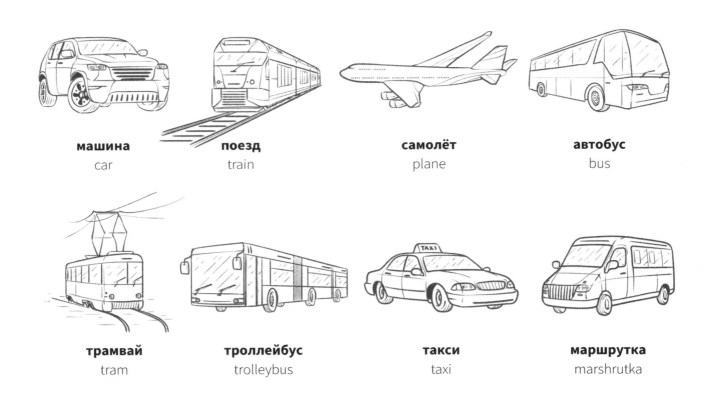

машина
car

поезд
train

самолёт
plane

автобус
bus

трамвай
tram

троллейбус
trolleybus

такси
taxi

маршрутка
marshrutka

🔊 OTHER USEFUL WORDS

билет (на) + accusative	ticket (for)
багаж	luggage
сумка	bag
чемодан паковать чемодан(ы)	suitcase to pack a suitcase(s)
кошелёк	purse/wallet
деньги (на) + accusative	money (for)
карточка расплатиться карточкой/наличными	card (for payments) to pay with card/in cash
номер	hotel room or number

ключ (от) + genitive	key (to)
прохожий	passerby
администратор	receptionist
экскурсовод	guide
карта города	city map
сувенир	souvenir
подарок	present
путешествие/путешественник отправиться в путешествие	travel/traveler to go on a trip
информация	information
турист привлекать туристов	tourist to attract tourists
туристическое агентство	tourist agency
вход в	entrance (to)
выход из	exit (out of)
лифт работает/не работает	elevator works/doesn't work

 *The difference between the verbs 'идти - ходить', 'ехать-ездить', and 'бежать - бегать'

Идти, ехать, бежать	Ходить, ездить, бегать
Go, go by vehicle, run	
Single-time action and direction in a single movement, which means that the action is taking place now. Я **иду** на работу. – I'm going to work. Я **еду** на велосипеде. – I'm riding a bike. Я **бегу** на автобус. – I'm running to catch the bus.	Regularly repeated action, happens in present but not at the moment of speech. Я **хожу** в школу с другом. – I go to school with a friend. Я **езжу** на рынок на автобусе. – I go to the market by bus. Я **бегаю** очень медленно. – I run very slowly.

QUESTIONS AND SAMPLE ANSWERS

When asking strangers for directions, start with '**скажите, пожалуйста**' or '**не могли бы вы сказать**', which is the Russian equivalent for 'could you please tell me'.

Question	Sample Answer
Где находится вокзал? Where is the railway station?	**Вокзал находится на улице Ленина.** The railway station is in Lenina street.
На каком автобусе я могу доехать до почты? Which bus can take me to the post office?	**Вы можете доехать до почты на двадцать третьем автобусе.** Bus number 23 can get you to the post office.
Как я могу добраться до аэропорта? How can I get to the airport?	**Вы можете поехать на метро или можете взять такси.** You can go by underground or you can take a taxi.
Как пройти до супермаркета? How can I get to the supermarket?	**Идите* до светофора, а потом поверните налево.** Go to the traffic lights and then turn left.
Где я могу купить билет на троллейбус? Where can I buy a ticket for the trolleybus?	**Вы можете купить билет в этом киоске.** You can buy tickets at this stand.
Могу я забронировать номер на среду? Can I book a room for Wednesday?	**Да, конечно! Ваше имя и фамилия, пожалуйста.** Yes, of course! Your name and last name, please.
Как я могу вызвать такси? How can I call a taxi?	**Позвоните по номеру 6688.** Call number 6688.

 *Unlike in English, in Russian we use ordinal numerals for the number of floors, hotel rooms, buses, etc.

Example: Я поеду на **третьем** автобусе. – I'll go on bus **three**.

 *When giving instructions and directions to others, you need to know how to form the imperative case. However, this rule involves a lot of grammar-related material, so for now we suggest you just remember the forms for some of the topic-related verbs. Here are the forms for the 2nd person singular and plural.

иди/идите	go
поверни/поверните	turn
перейди/перейдите	cross
сядь/сядьте	get on
возьми/возьмите	take

PREPOSITIONS OF PLACE AND MOVEMENT*

1) В – in, at + prepositional case. Indicates that the object is inside something.

В номере очень жарко! – It's very hot **in** the room!

Я купила этот сувенир **в** супермаркет**е**. – I've bought this souvenir **at** the supermarket.

2) На – on, at + prepositional case. Normally indicates that the object is situated on a flat surface.

Ключи от машины **на** столе. – The keys to the car are on the table.

There are cases that may seem to be not that obvious:

на остановке – at a (bus) station

на улице (+ street name) – on a street (on Pushkina street)

на станции – at a station

на площади – at a square

на почте – at a post office

на углу – at the corner

на светофоре – at the traffic lights

на перекрёстке – at the crossroads

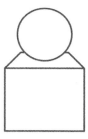

3) Под – under + instrumental case

Мы нашли щенка **под** мост**ом**. – We've found a puppy **under** the bridge.

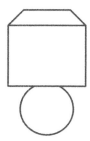

4) За – behind + instrumental case

Кафе находится **за** кинотеатр**ом**. – The café is **behind** the cinema.

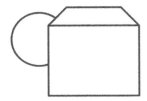

5) Перед – in front of + instrumental case

Я жду тебя **перед** банк**ом**. – I'm waiting for you **in front of** the bank.

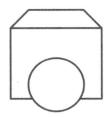

6) Над – above + instrumental case

Аптека находится прямо **над** книжн**ым** магазин**ом**. – The drugstore is right **above** the book store.

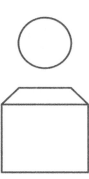

7) Около, возле – next to, near + genitive case

Банк находится **около** центральн**ого** парк**а**. – The bank is **next to** the central park.

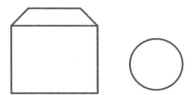

8) Между – between + instrumental case

Торговый центр находится **между** банк**ом** и школ**ой**. – The mall is **between** the bank and the school.

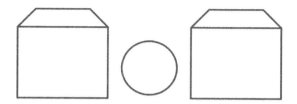

9) Слева/справа от – to the left/right of + genitive case

Парковка находится **справа от** площад**и** Побед**ы**. – The parking lot is **to the right of** Victory Square.

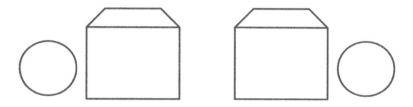

10) Напротив – opposite + genitive case

Полиция находится **напротив** автостанц**ии**. – The police station is opposite the bus station.

11) Идти до – to go up to + genitive case

Идите прямо до светофора, а потом поверните направо. – Go straight ahead up to the traffic lights and then turn right.

12) Идти вдоль – to go along + genitive case

Идите **вдоль** парк**а** и поверните направо возле аптек**и**. – Go **along** the park and turn left near the drugstore.

* See the rule for case forms in the Grammar Appendix (page 185).

THE VERB 'МОЧЬ-CAN' IN PRESENT TENSE

Being a very important verb, 'мочь' has an irregular conjugation pattern, while its infinitive form is never used. Remember these forms:

Я могу	**Вы** можете
Ты можешь	**Он/она/оно** может
Мы можем	**Они** могут

Example: Вы **можете** пересесть на этой станции. – You **can** change trains at this station.

THE PAST TENSE IN RUSSIAN

In Russian, the past tense is needed to talk about past events. Being able to conjugate the verbs properly is a large part of learning the vocabulary and grammar. The good news is that the conjugation of verbs in the past tense is so easy that we've placed it here instead of the Grammar Appendix.

The ending depends on the gender of subject, i.e., the doer of the action. To conjugate a verb in the past tense, remove the ending '-ть' from the initial form and add:

Masculine	**-л**
купить – to buy Папа (он) купил продукты на рынке. – Dad (he) bought groceries at the market.	
Feminine	**-ла**
приехать – to come by vehicle Моя сестра (она) приехала сюда на поезде. – My sister (she) came here by train.	
Neutral	**-ло**
прийти – to arrive Письмо (оно) пришло утром. – The letter (it) arrived in the morning.	
Plural	**-ли**
фотографировать – to take photos Туристы фотографировали собор. – The tourists (they) were taking photos of the cathedral.	

The words that can help you understand that the action took place in the past:

вчера – yesterday

позавчера – the day before yesterday

в прошлом году – last year

на прошлой неделе – last week

в прошлом месяце – last month

в детстве – in my childhood

THE VERBS 'БЫТЬ' AND 'ЕСТЬ' IN THE PAST TENSE

As you know, the verb 'to be - быть' is omitted in the present tense; however, in the past tense it's obligatory.

For example: Дом справа от банка. – The house **is** to the right of the bank.

Дом **был** справа от банка. – The house **was** to the right of the bank.

In constructions 'Здесь есть' – 'There is/are' and 'У меня есть – I've got' 'есть' is replaced with the corresponding past form. The conjugation of these verbs in the past is irregular.

Example: У меня **есть** билеты в театр. – **I've got** tickets to the theater.

У меня **были** билеты в театр. – I **had** tickets to the theater.

Masculine – был В двадцать лет он **был** студентом. – At twenty he **was a** student.
Feminine – была В детстве у меня **была** любимая игрушка. – During my childhood, I **had** a favorite toy.
Neutral – было Солнце **было** высоко. – The sun **was** high.
Plural – были В комнате **были** дети и их родители. – There **were** children and their parents in the room.

CONJUGATION OF IRREGULAR VERBS OF MOTION

Many verbs of motion are conjugated in an irregular pattern, so we've placed them here for you to remember and use correctly.

Present tense

	я	ты	мы	вы	он/она/оно	они
(при)ехать	(при)езжаю	(при)езжаешь	(при)езжаем	(при)езжаете	(при)езжает	(при)езжают
ездить	езжу	ездишь	ездим	ездите	ездит	ездят
садиться	сажусь	садишься	садимся	садитесь	садится	садятся
сойти	схожу	сходишь	сходим	сходите	сходит	сходят
выйти	выхожу	выходишь	выходим	выходите	выходит	выходят
войти	вхожу	входишь	входим	входите	входит	входят
летать	(при)летаю	(при)летаешь	(при)летаем	(при)летаете	(при)летает	(при)летают
идти	иду	идёшь	идём	идёте	идёт	идут
бежать	бегу	бежишь	бежим	бежите	бежит	бегут

Past tense

	Masculine	Feminine	Neutral	Plural
(при)ехать	(при)ехал	(при)ехала	(при)ехало	приехали
ездить	ездил	ездила	ездило	ездили
садиться	сел	села	село	сели
сойти	сошёл	сошла	сошло	сошли
выйти	вышел	вышла	вышло	вышли
войти	вошёл	вошла	вошло	вошли
идти	шёл	шла	шло	шли
лететь	(при)летел	(при)летела	(при)летело	(при)летели
бежать	бежал	бежала	бежало	бежали

📝 EXERCISES

01. Find the following objects on the map and write the corresponding number as your answer.

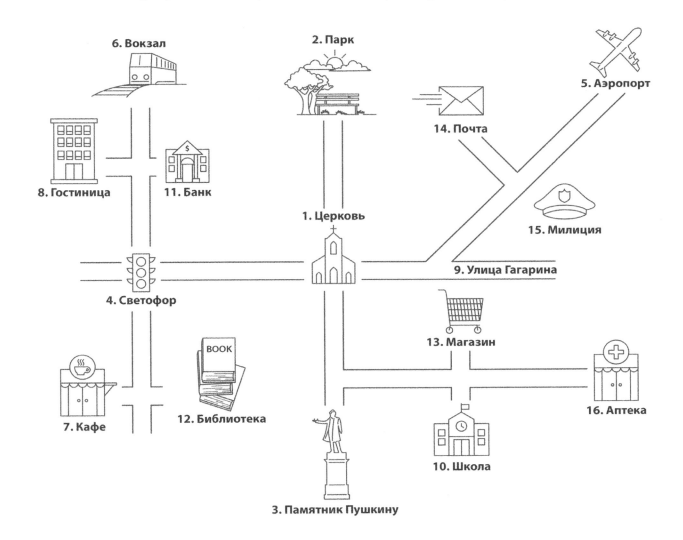

6. Вокзал
2. Парк
5. Аэропорт
14. Почта
8. Гостиница
11. Банк
1. Церковь
15. Милиция
9. Улица Гагарина
4. Светофор
13. Магазин
16. Аптека
7. Кафе
12. Библиотека
10. Школа
3. Памятник Пушкину

(　　) **1)** Railway station　　　　(　　) **9)** School

(　　) **2)** Airport　　　　(　　) **10)** Park

(　　) **3)** Shop　　　　(　　) **11)** Monument to Pushkin

(　　) **4)** Café　　　　(　　) **12)** Gagarina street

(　　) **5)** Post office　　　　(　　) **13)** Church

(　　) **6)** Library　　　　(　　) **14)** Traffic lights

(　　) **7)** Bank　　　　(　　) **15)** Hotel

(　　) **8)** Police station　　　　(　　) **16)** Drugstore

02. Complete these sentences with the right prepositions of place. Use the map from Exercise 1.

Sample: Памятник Пушкину находится **напротив** церкви. – A monument to Pushkin is opposite the church.

1) Церковь находится _____ парком и памятником.

2) Магазин находится _____ улице Гагарина.

3) Аптека находится справа _____ школы.

4) Деревья находятся _____ парке.

5) Парк находится _____ церковью.

6) Библиотека находится слева _____ памятника.

03. Use the map. Imagine you're standing behind Pushkin's monument with your back to it. Listen to the instructions and tell us what object they lead you to. If something is too hard for you, listen to the English version of the instructions.

04. Change your location on the map and create similar instructions. Get your partner to guess what object they lead to.

05. Match these nouns with the images.

1) Билет

2) Номер

3) Кошелёк

4) Деньги

5) Лифт

6) Карточка

7) Вход

8) Выход

9) Ключ

10) Прохожий

A) (   )   B) (   )   C) (   )   D) (   )   E) (   )

F) (   )   G) (   )   H) (   )   I) (   )   J) (   )

06. Fill in these sentences with the words from previous exercises. Remember to use them in the right case forms.

1) Извините, где находится _____в кинотеатр?

2) Я не могу найти _____от нашего номера!

3) Сколько _____мне нужно на билеты?

4) Мы заблудились! Давай спросим дорогу у _____.

5) Здравствуйте! Я бы хотел забронировать _____на вторник.

6) Это не мой _____. Мой красный, а этот белый.

7) О, нет! _____не работает!

8) Я уже купила (bought) _____на поезд.

9) Где _____из этого магазина?

10) Я могу расплатиться _____?

07. Match the columns to make expressions from the vocabulary list and write them under the corresponding images.

( ) **1)** паковать	**A)** такси
( ) **2)** спросить	**B)** дорогу
( ) **3)** вызывать	**C)** чемоданы
( ) **4)** фотографировать	**D)** выставки
( ) **5)** переходить	**E)** дорогу
( ) **6)** посещать	**F)** достопримечательности

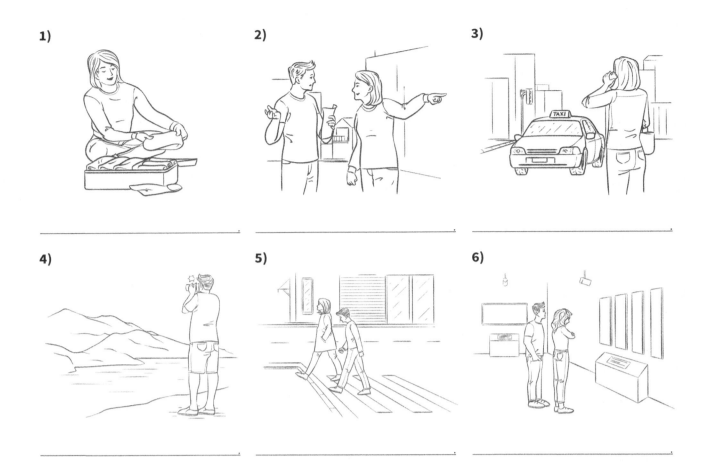

1)

2)

3)

4)

5)

6)

08. Fill in the verbs from exercise 7 in past tense.

1) Туристы (фотографировать) достопримечательности и (посещать) выставки. Им очень понравилась экскурсия!
The tourists were taking photos of the sights and exhibitions they visited. They liked the excursion a lot!

2) Мой брат спешил и (вызвать) такси.
My brother was in a hurry and called a taxi.

3) Пешеход (переходить) дорогу, когда светофор был красным.
The pedestrian was crossing the road when the traffic lights were red.

4) Мы (паковать) чемоданы два часа! Надеюсь, мы ничего не забыли!
We've been packing the suitcases for two hours! Hope we didn't forget anything!

5) Я (спросить) дорогу у прохожего.
I asked a passerby for directions.

09. Match the verbs with the correct case forms of nouns that define means of transport.

( ) **1)** ехать/приехать to go/to come or to arrive by	**A)** с самолёт**а**
( ) **2)** садиться to get on/into	**B)** на самолёт**е**
( ) **3)** сойти to get off	**C)** в автобус/машин**у**/поезд/маршрутк**у**/трамвай/троллейбус
( ) **4)** выйти to get off/out of	**D)** на автобус**е**/машин**е**/поезд**е**/маршрутк**е**/трамва**е**/троллейбус**е** OR атобус**ом**/машин**ой**/поезд**ом**/маршрутк**ой**/трамва**ем**/троллейбус**ом**
( ) **5)** лететь to fly by	**E)** из автобус**а**/машин**ы**/поезд**а**/маршрутк**и**/трамва**я**/троллейбус**а**

10. Read these texts in which people describe their way to a destination. Fill in the right forms of the verbs of motion.

Text I

Меня зовут Лена. Мой университет далеко от моего дома. Сначала я **1) (садиться)** _____

на атобус и **2) (ехать)** _____ до метро. Затем я **3) (выходить)** _____

из автобуса и **4) (садиться)** _____ на метро. После метро я **5) (ехать)** _____

на трамвае и потом иду пешком десять минут. Но вчера мне повезло. Моя подруга **6) (ехать)** _____
на машине и подвезла меня.

My name is Lena. My university is far away from my home. Firstly, I get on a bus and get off at the subway. Then I get out of the bus and take the subway. After the subway, I go by streetcar and then go on foot for ten minutes. But yesterday I was lucky. My friend was driving, and she gave me a lift.

Text 2

Меня зовут Андрей. Вчера я был в Москве по работе. Я живу в Екатеринбурге, поэтому дорога была

длинной. Сначала я **1) (лететь)** _____ на самолёте всю ночь. Утром я

2) (сойти) _____ с самолёта и **3) (взять)** _____ такси до офиса. Но на

дороге была пробка. Я **4) (выйти)** _____ из такси и **5) (садиться)** _____

на метро. Я **6) (выйти)** _____ из метро, но это была не та станция! Я снова **7) (войти)**

_____ в метро и **8) (ехать)** _____ ещё две станции!

My name is Andrey. Yesterday I was in Moscow on business. I live in Yekaterinburg, so the trip was long. First, I flew by plane the whole night. In the morning I got off the plane and took a taxi to the office. But there was a traffic jam on the road. I got out of the taxi and took the subway. I got out of the subway but it was the wrong station! I took the subway again and rode it for two more stations!

11. Go back to exercise 10 and change the verbs according to

a) 3rd person singular (she)

Text 1 _____.

Text 2 _____.

b) 3rd person plural (they)

Text 1 _____.

Text 2 _____.

c) 2nd person singular (you)

Text 1 _____.

Text 2 _____.

Check your work with the table in the vocabulary section.

12. Practice the difference between the pairs of verbs 'ходить-идти', 'ездить-ехать', and 'бежать-бегать'. Underline the correct variant.

1) Я не могу говорить с тобой сейчас. Я **бегу/бегаю** на работу.
I can't talk to you now. I'm running to work.

2) Она **бегает/бежит** каждое утро.
She runs every morning.

3) Мы **ездим/едем** на работу на автобусе.
We go to work by bus.

4) Дети не **ходят/идут** в школу летом.
Children don't go to school in summer.

5) Куда он **бежит/бегает**?
Where is he running?

6) Вы сегодня **ездите/едете** на такси или на метро?
Are you going by taxi or by subway today?

7) Я **иду/хожу** в магазин. Что тебе купить?
I'm going to the shop. What should I buy you?

8) Мой дедушка **ходит/идёт** на прогулку каждый вечер.
My grandfather goes for a walk every evening.

9) Почему вы **бежите/бегаете**? Вы опаздываете?
Why are you running? Are you late?

10) Они **ездят/едут** за город каждые выходные.
They go to the country every weekend.

13. Match the questions with the answers.

( ) **1)** Где я могу купить сувениры для своей семьи?	**A)** Конечно! Назовите свою фамилию, пожалуйста!
( ) **2)** Как я могу добраться до больницы?	**B)** Вон там, между парком и аптекой.
( ) **3)** Где я могу купить билеты на поезд?	**C)** Нет, десятый автобус не ходит до театра. Садитесь на второй автобус.
( ) **4)** Могу я забронировать номер на четверг?	**D)** Вы можете купить сувениры в магазине за углом.
( ) **5)** Скажите, пожалуйста, где находится банк?	**E)** Вы можете купить билеты на вокзале.
( ) **6)** Я могу доехать до театра на десятом автобусе?	**F)** Вы можете сесть на пятый трамвай или поехать на метро.

14. Imagine you were asked the questions from exercise 14 in your home city. How would you answer them? Use the above answers as the structure and just replace with your own information.

15. Fill in the conversations with the words from the box using them in the right tense and case forms. Pay attention to the useful expressions in bold. Listen to the conversations and roleplay them after checking your work.

Conversation I

Тебе понравилось путешествие? – Did you like the trip?

> музеи вернуться дискотеки приехать экскурсовод отель
> достопримечательности наслаждаться

A: Привет, София! Вы уже **1)** _____из путешествия?

B: Да, Света, мы **2)** _____домой два дня назад.

A: Вам понравилось в Новгороде?

B: Да, очень! Мы **3)** _____каждым днём!

A: Рада это слышать! Вы остановились у твоих родственников?

B: Нет, мы заселились в **4)** _____.

A: Ясно. Что тебе понравилось больше всего?

B: Мне очень понравились экскурсии. **5)** _____рассказал много интересного о городе.

A: О, я знаю, ты любишь **6)** _____, **выставки и всё такое.** А там есть ночные клубы

или **7)** _____?

B: Думаю, да, но мы осматривали **8)** _____, а не клубы.

A: Hi Sofia! Have you already returned from the trip?

B: Yes, Sveta, we came home two days ago.

A: Did you like it in Novgorod?

B: Yes, a lot! We enjoyed every day!

A: Glad to hear it! Did you stay with your relatives'?

B: No, we checked into a hotel.

A: I see. What did you like most of all?

B: I liked the excursions a lot. The guide told us so many interesting things about the city.

A: Oh, I know you like museums, **exhibitions and such stuff**. And are there any nightclubs or discos there?

B: I guess there are, but we did the sights, not the clubs.

Conversation II

Это был кошмар! – That was a nightmare!

> аэропорт за багаж деньги номер путешествие взять
> администратор кошелёк

A: Мне не понравилось моё **1)** _____ !

B: Как жаль! Почему?

A: Сначала я потерял свой **2)** _____ в **3)** _____.

B: Ты или работники аэропорта?

A: Я. Я забыл его в туалете. Затем я **4)** _____ такси до гостиницы. Я хотел заплатить **5)** _____ такси, но я потерял свой **6)** _____.

B: О, нет! Как ты заплатил за такси?

A: У меня было немного **7)** _____ в кармане. **8)** _____ в отеле помог мне. Он позвонил в аэропорт, они проверили туалет. Мой кошелёк был там.

B: Слава Богу! Но тебе понравился город?

A: Да. Но потом я потерял ключ от **9)** _____.

B: Ты что, шутишь?

A: Ах, если бы!

A: I didn't like my trip!

B: What a pity! Why?

A: First, I lost my luggage at the airport.

B: Was it you or an employee of the airport?

A: It was me. I forgot it in the restroom. Then I took a taxi to the hotel. I wanted to pay for the taxi, but I lost my wallet.

B: Oh, no! How did you pay for the taxi?

A: I had some money in my pocket. The receptionist at the hotel helped. He called the airport, they checked the restrooms. My wallet was there.

B: Thank God! But did you like the city?

A: I did. But then I lost the key to the hotel room.

B: Are you kidding me?

A: I wish I was!

UNIT IV
DESCRIBING THINGS

This unit features the vocabulary you'll need to describe weather, people's appearance and character, as well as to ask and answer the related questions. Since these topics feature less vocabulary and few grammar constructions (that are also interrelated), we've included them in one unit and divided it into three parts.

PART I - DESCRIBING APPEARANCE

VOCABULARY

📢 Моя подруга - My friend

Моя подруга Аня очень **красивая** девушка. Она **высокая** и **стройная**. У неё **длинные русые волосы** и **большие голубые глаза**. Но ей не нравится её **внешность**! Она говорит, что у неё **короткие ресницы** и **слишком тонкие губы**.

My friend Anya is a very **beautiful** girl. She's **tall** and **slim**. She's got **long fair hair** and **big blue eyes**. But she doesn't like her **appearance**! She says she's got **short eyelashes** and **too-thin lips**.

Это странно. Я всегда говорю Ане, что она красивая. Мои волосы **короткие** и тонкие, мои **щёки немного пухлые**, а мой нос слишком **маленький**. Но я всё равно красивая! Все люди красивые! Вы согласны со мной?

It's strange. I always tell Anya that she's beautiful. My hair is **short** and thin, my **cheeks are a bit plump** and my nose is too **small**. But I am beautiful no matter what! All people are beautiful! Do you agree with me?

📢 PARTS OF THE BODY AND OTHER NOUNS

тело	body
голова	head
лицо	face
глаз/глаза	eye/eyes
ресницы	eyelashes
брови	brows
нос	nose
губа/губы	lip/lips
рот	mouth
зуб/зубы	tooth/teeth
щека/щёки	cheek/cheeks
подбородок	chin
борода	beard
усы	mustache
ухо/уши	ear/ears
шея	neck
плечо/плечи	shoulder/s
рука/руки	hand/arm/hands/arms

палец/пальцы	finger/fingers (both for hands and feet)
локоть	elbow
грудь	chest
живот	belly
талия	waist
бёдра	hips
нога/ноги	leg/legs
стопа/стопы	foot/feet
рост	height
вес	weight
внешность	appearance

🔊 ADJECTIVES FOR DESCRIPTION

красивый	beautiful (both for males and females)
привлекательный	attractive
молодой	young
пожилой	elderly
средних лет	middle-aged
большой	big
маленький	small
средний	medium
длинный	long
короткий	short
стройный	slim
толстый	fat (about weight)
худой	skinny
густой	thick
тонкий	thin
полный	stout
пухлый	plump
высокий	tall
низкий	short
среднего роста	of medium height
прямой	straight
вьющийся	curly
лысый	bald
узкий	narrow
широкий	wide

тёмный	dark
светлый	fair
чёрный	black
рыжий	red (about hair)
белый	white
русый	brown
тёмно-русый	deep brown
светло-русый	light brown
карий	brown (about eyes)
зелёный	green
синий	deep blue
голубой	light blue

 Unlike in English, there is no adjective for 'blond' in Russian. Instead, the nouns 'блондин' and 'блондинка' are used, which could be translated as 'a man with blond hair' and 'a woman with blond hair'.

Compare: Она блондинка. – She's got blond hair.

HOW TO USE NOUNS WITH ADJECTIVES TO MAKE DESCRIPTIONS

Just like nouns, adjectives change according to gender, number, and case, but for now we'll only learn how to correlate adjectives with nouns in the nominative case. Masculine singular nominative is considered to be the initial form of an adjective.

So, to describe any part of appearance or any other thing, we can use the following patterns:

1) Adjective + noun
Красив**ая** девушка – a beautiful girl

2) Noun + adjective
Эта девушка красив**ая**. – This girl is beautiful.

The form of an adjective depends on the form of a noun it's related to.

ADJECTIVES IN THE NOMINATIVE CASE

1) Adjectives that have 'hard' endings (-ый, -ой, -ий (but not -ний))

Masculine	-ый, -ой, -ий
нов**ый** дом – new house молод**ой** человек – young man высок**ий** парень – tall guy	
Feminine	**-ая**
нов**ая** машина – new car молод**ая** девушка – young girl высок**ая** женщина – tall woman	
Neutral	**-ое**
нов**ое** пальто – new coat молод**ое** дерево – young tree высок**ое** здание – high building	
Plural	**-ые**
нов**ые** книги – new books молод**ые** люди – young people высок**ие*** здания – high buildings	

*According to spelling rules, 'к' is never followed by 'ы', so the letter is changed.

2) Adjectives that end in -ний

Masculine	-ний
си**ний** дом – blue house	
Feminine	**-яя**
син**яя** птица – blue bird	
Neutral	**-ее**
син**ее** пальто – blue coat	
Plural	**-ие**
син**ие** здания – blue buildings	

 Although these are the forms of the nominative case, you can also use them with the accusative case, because accusative forms of inanimate nouns correspond to the forms of the nominative case. See the Grammar Appendix pages 179-180.

This hack is rather useful for describing appearance, since one of the most common patterns includes the forms of the accusative case.

> ### У меня голубые глаза – I've got blue eyes
> У + personal pronoun in genitive + adjective + noun (both in accusative)

 Also , note a few more patterns:

Он высокого/среднего/низкого роста – He's tall/of medium height/short

But you can also say: Он высокий/низкий (not 'он средний'! This adjective works only with the word 'роста' in this context.)

Она молодая/среднего возраста/пожилая – She's young/middle-aged/elderly

You can also say: Она женщина среднего/пожилого возраста – She's a woman of a middle/elderly age.

How to say you had something in the past?

As you know, the Russian equivalent for **'I've got' is 'У меня есть'.** The past tense construction requires the past form of the verb 'быть' or 'есть'. See the conjugation on page 107.

Example:

У меня **были** длинные волосы.
I used to have long hair.

У тебя **была** верная собака.
You **used to have** a loyal dog.

To say that you DID NOT have something, always use the form 'было' no matter the gender of the noun.

У него **не было** усов. – He didn't have a mustache (plural).

У неё **не было** машины. – She didn't have a car (feminine).

У нас **не было** ребёнка. – We didn't have a child (masculine).

QUESTIONS AND SAMPLE ANSWERS

Какого* цвета у тебя волосы? (у + personal pronoun in the genitive case) **Какого цвета твои волосы?** What is the color of your hair?	**Мои волосы рыжие.** My hair is red. **У меня рыжие волосы.** I've got red hair.
Какого Вы/ты роста? **Какой у Вас/тебя рост?** What is your height?	**Я среднего роста.** I'm of medium height. **Я высокая.** I'm tall. **Мой рост сто семьдесят сантиметров.** My height is one hundred and seventy centimeters.
Сколько Вы весите (ты весишь)? How much do you weigh? **Какой у Вас (тебя) вес?** What is your weight?	**Я вешу семьдесят пять килограмм.** I weigh seventy-five kilos. **Мой вес девяносто два килограмма.** My weight is ninety-two kilos.

*In the words that end in -ого, the letter 'г' is read like the English 'v'.

📑 EXERCISES

01. Look at the picture and write down the corresponding words in the column. You can rely on your memory and then check yourself with the vocabulary section. Make sure to use both singular and plural forms, where applicable.

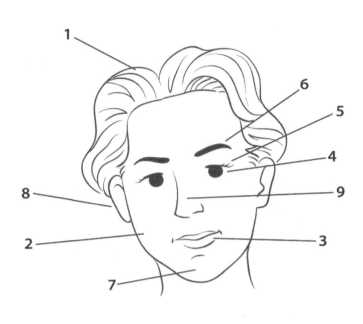

1) _____.

2) _____.

3) _____.

4) _____.

5) _____.

6) _____.

7) _____.

8) _____.

9) _____.

02. Do the same as in the previous exercise.

1) _____.

2) _____.

3) _____.

4) _____.

5) _____.

6) _____.

7) _____.

8) _____.

9) _____.

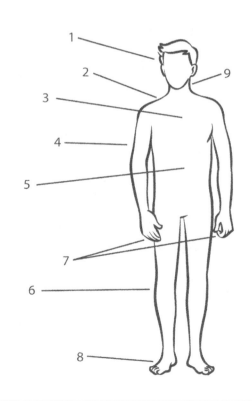

03. Match the columns to form pairs of antonyms. Then use the table in the vocabulary section to make these adjectives feminine.

(   ) **1)** стройный _____ .   **A)** высокий _____ .

(   ) **2)** большой _____ .   **B)** вьющийся _____ .

(   ) **3)** низкий _____ .   **C)** пожилой _____ .

(   ) **4)** длинный _____ .   **D)** толстый _____ .

(   ) **5)** молодой _____ .   **E)** светлый _____ .

(   ) **6)** тёмный _____ .   **F)** некрасивый _____ .

(   ) **7)** прямой _____ .   **G)** маленький _____ .

(   ) **8)** красивый _____ .   **H)** короткий _____ .

04. Put the words in the correct order to make sentences.

1) подруги/густые/у/волосы/длинные/моей.

_____ .

2) внешность/не/мне/моя/нравится.

_____ .

3) мамы/какого/Вашей/цвета/волосы/у?

_____ .

4) мужа/у/моего/бороды/нет.

_____ .

5) парня/у/голубые/твоего/или/глаза/карие?

_____ .

6) сколько/кот/весит/твой?

_____ .

7) что/она/уши/говорит/большие/неё/у.

_____ .

8) подбородок/толстый/мужчины/у/был

_____ .

05. Create descriptions based on these forms. Then fill in the last form to describe yourself.

А)

> **Имя:** Марина
>
> **Возраст:** 25 лет
>
> **Рост:** 175 см, высокая
>
> **Вес:** 87 кг
>
> **Глаза:** зелёные
>
> **Нос:** прямой
>
> **Волосы:** блондинка, вьющиеся, короткие
>
> **Ресницы:** длинные
>
> **Пальцы:** тонкие

_____

_____

_____

_____

_____ .

В)

> **Имя:** Арсений
>
> **Возраст:** 40 лет
>
> **Рост:** 169 см
>
> **Вес:** 65 кг
>
> **Глаза:** голубые
>
> **Волосы:** короткие, прямые
>
> **Борода:** нет
>
> **Губы:** тонкие

_____

_____

_____

_____

_____ .

С)

> **Имя:**
>
> **Возраст:**
>
> **Рост:**
>
> **Вес:**
>
> **Глаза:**
>
> **Волосы:**
>
> **Губы:**
>
> **Ресницы:**

_____

_____

_____

_____

_____ .

06. Compare these people at different ages according to the sample.

Sample: В двадцать лет у меня были рыжие волосы. Сейчас я блондинка.

At twenty I had red hair. I've got blond hair now.

Person	Time in the past/appearance	Now/appearance
1) Твоя мама	в прошлом году/полная	стройная
2) Мой брат	в двадцать лет/густые волосы	лысый
3) Ваши дети	в детстве/светло-русые волосы	тёмно-русые волосы
4) Я	в пятнадцать лет/вьющиеся волосы	прямые волосы
5) Наш дядя	в школе/очень высокий	среднего роста

1) _____ .

2) _____ .

3) _____ .

4) _____ .

5) _____ .

07. Listen to the texts and match them with the images.

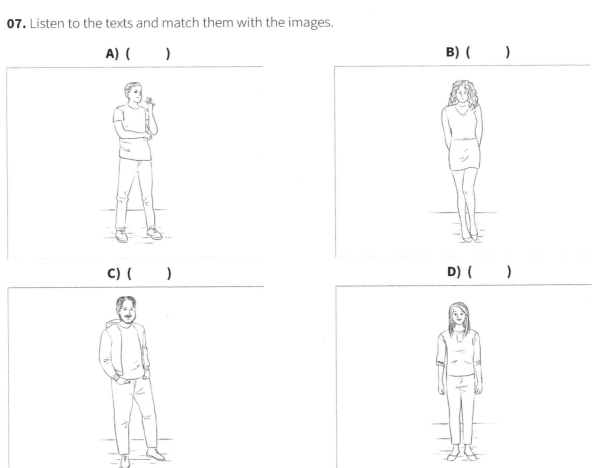

A) (   )

B) (   )

C) (   )

D) (   )

PART II - DESCRIBING CHARACTER

VOCABULARY

📢 Мой ужасный характер - My horrible character

Все мои **родственники** говорят, что у меня **ужасный** характер. Я не согласен! Да, я **вспыльчивый**, но я быстро успокаиваюсь. Да, я **немного ленивый**, но я хожу на работу и много зарабатываю. Разве это плохо?

All my **relatives** say that I've got a **horrible** character. I don't agree! Yes, I'm **hot-tempered,** but I **calm down** quickly. Yes, I'm a bit **lazy**, but I go to work and earn a lot. Is that bad?

Я не **злой** человек. Наоборот, я очень **добрый** и помогаю семье и друзьям. Да, иногда я **скучный** и не очень **эмоциональный**. Это не плохо. Моя двоюродная сестра, например, **слишком энергичная**. И всем это нравится! Но не мне. По крайней мере, моя девушка говорит, что я **романтичный** и **надёжный**.

I'm not an **evil** person. On the contrary, I'm very **kind** and help my family and friends. Yes, I'm **boring** sometimes and not very **emotional**. That's not bad! My cousin is too **energetic**, for example. And everybody likes it! But not me. At least my girlfriend says that I'm **romantic** and **reliable**.

📢 CHARACTER TRAITS

добрый доброта	kind kindness
злой	evil
эмоциональный эмоциональность	emotional emotionality
вспыльчивый	hot-tempered
раздражительный раздражаться	irritable get irritated
энергичный	energetic
спокойный	calm
дружелюбный дружелюбность	friendly friendliness

трудолюбивый	hard-working
ленивый	lazy
лентяй/лентяйка	lazy person (masculine/feminine)
лень	laziness
умный	smart
глупый	silly
глупость	silliness
тупой	stupid
крутой	cool
креативный	creative
скучный	boring
весёлый	fun, easygoing
честный	honest
честность	honesty
капризный	moody
надёжный	reliable
надёжность	reliability
(без)ответственный	(ir)responsible
(без)ответственность	(ir)responsibility
романтичный	romantic
эгоистичный	selfish
застенчивый	shy
застенчивость	shyness
уверенный в себе	self-confident
серьёзный	serious
сильный	strong
слабый	weak
достоинство/а	advantage/s
недостаток/недостатки	drawback/s (flaw/s)

PATTERNS FOR DESCRIBING YOURSELF AND OTHER PEOPLE

> **Я ленивый – I'm lazy**
> Personal pronoun + adjective (both in nominative)

> **У неё спокойный характер – She's got a calm character**
> У + personal pronoun in genitive + adjective in nominative + характер

📢 QUESTIONS AND SAMPLE ANSWERS

Какой у тебя/Вас характер? **Какой ты/Вы по характеру?** What kind of character have you got?	**Я энергичный.** I'm energetic. **У меня энергичный характер.** **По характеру я энергичный.** I've got an energetic character.
У тебя есть недостатки? Have you got flaws?	**Да, у меня есть недостатки. Я немного застенчивая.** Yes, I've got flaws. I'm a bit shy.
Какой твой главный недостаток? What is your major flaw?	**Иногда я очень ленивый.** I'm very lazy sometimes.
Какое твоё главное достоинство? What is your major advantage?	**Я трудолюбивая и ответственная.** I'm hardworking and responsible.

 The question word **'какой' – 'what, what kind of, which'** is declined according to number, gender and case, and its endings correspond to that of adjectives ending in -ой.

Example: Как**ой** характер у твоего сына? – What kind of character has your son got?

Как**ая** она по характеру? – What kind of character has she got?

Как**ое** мороженое ты хочешь? – Which/what kind of ice-cream do you want?

Как**ие** книги тебе нравятся? – What kind of books do you like?

📑 Exercises

01. Match these adjectives with the images.

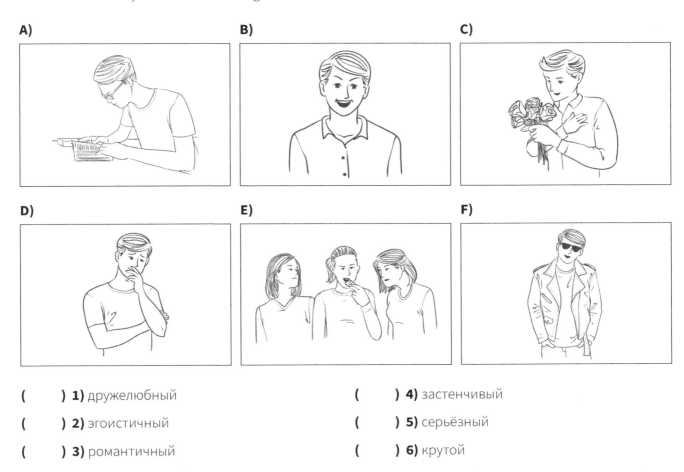

A)   **B)**   **C)**

D)   **E)**   **F)**

(   ) **1)** дружелюбный   (   ) **4)** застенчивый

(   ) **2)** эгоистичный   (   ) **5)** серьёзный

(   ) **3)** романтичный   (   ) **6)** крутой

02. Match the words in the columns to create pairs of antonyms.

( ) **1)** креативный	**A)** злой
( ) **2)** вспыльчивый	**B)** безответственный
( ) **3)** добрый	**C)** уверенный в себе
( ) **4)** трудолюбивый	**D)** слабый
( ) **5)** надёжный	**E)** спокойный
( ) **6)** застенчивый	**F)** скучный
( ) **7)** сильный	**G)** глупый
( ) **8)** умный	**H)** ленивый

	Достоинство	Недостаток	Нравится в людях	Не нравится в людях
Лена				
Саша				
Дима				
Настя				

04. Answer the following questions based on the table from Exercise 3. The questions and answers for Lena are given as a sample. Do the same for others and write down your answers.

Sample:

1) Лена, какое твоё главное достоинство?

Я креативная.

2) Какой твой главный недостаток?

Мой главный недостаток – лень/я ленивая.

3) Что тебе нравится в людях?

Мне нравится честность/мне нравятся честные люди.

4) Какие люди тебе не нравятся?

Мне не нравятся злые люди.

_____

_____

_____

_____

_____

_____

_____

_____

_____

05. Answer the questions from Exercise 5 for yourself. Ask your partner the questions from the Q&A table (questions and answers) in the vocabulary section, then ask them to do the same for you. You can also ask questions about their friends and family.

PART III - DESCRIBING WEATHER

VOCABULARY

📢 **Прекрасная погода - Wonderful weather**

Сегодня прекрасный **солнечный** день. **На улице тепло** и нет **ветра**. **Небо ясное**. Мне нравится **такая погода**! Мы с друзьями пойдём на озеро, будем **купаться** и **загорать**.

Today is a wonderful **sunny** day. It's **warm outside** and there is no **wind**. **The sky is clear**. I like **such weather**. My friends and I will go to the lake, we'll be **swimming** and **sunbathing**.

Я обожаю **жару**! А моя мама **больше любит зиму**. Ей нравятся **морозные** дни. Ей нравится, когда **светит солнце** и **блестит снег**. Я не фанат зимы, но я люблю **Новый Год** и **Рождество**.

I love **heat**! And my mom **likes winter more**. She likes **frosty** days. She likes it when **the sun shines** and **the snow sparkles**. I'm not a fan of winter, but I like **New Year** and **Christmas**.

📢 **NOUNS DENOTING OBJECTS AND WEATHER-RELATED PHENOMENA**

солнце (светит)	the sun (is shining)
небо	sky
облако/облака	cloud/s
туча/тучи	thunder cloud/s
дождь идёт* дождь	rain it's raining/rains
снег (блестит) идёт снег	snow (is glittering) it's snowing
град идёт град	hail it's hailing
морось моросит	drizzle it's drizzling
жара	heat
мороз	frost
туман	fog

*the past form is 'шёл', for example: вчера шёл снег – it was snowing yesterday.

🔊 ADJECTIVES AND ADVERBS

дождливый/дождливо	rainy
солнечный/солнечно	sunny
тёплый/тепло	warm
горячий/горячо	hot
душный/душно	stuffy
холодный/холодно	cold
прохладный/прохладно	cool
морозный/морозно	frosty
снежный/снежно	snowy
туманный/туманно	foggy
ясный/ясно	clear
яркий/ярко	bright
сильный	heavy (about rain, snow, frost, hail)

PATTERNS TO TALK ABOUT WEATHER

На улице холодно. – It's cold outside.

На улице было холодно. – It was cold outside.

На улице + adverb in nominative

На улице + было + adverb in nominative

Сейчас (сегодня) тепло. – It's warm now (today).

Вчера было тепло. – It was warm yesterday.

Time in present + adverb in nominative

Time in the past + было + adverb in nominative

Pay attention to the form of the verb 'быть' in the past tense. In the constructions above, it's always 'было' and doesn't depend on anything, while in the constructions below the forms depend on the subject of the sentence.

Погода солнечная. – The weather is sunny.

Погода была солнечная. – The weather was sunny.

День жаркий. – The day is hot.

День был жаркий. – The day was hot.

Noun + adjective in nominative

Noun + быть in past tense + adjective in nominative

Example:

Feminine

Погода **была** солнечная.

The weather was sunny.

Masculine

День **был** солнечный.

The day was sunny.

Температура* минус (плюс) десять градусов**.

The temperature is minus (plus) ten degrees.

На улице минус (плюс) десять (градусов).

It's minus (plus) ten degrees outside.

---

*Russian people measure temperature in degrees Celsius.

**Depending on the numeral the word 'градусы' – 'degrees' can be 'градусов, градус, градуса'. The changes are similar to those with the noun 'лет' when talking about age (see page 20).

Какая твоя любимая погода? What is your favorite weather?	**Моя любимая погода морозная.** Frosty weather is my favorite.
Какая погода тебе нравится больше всего? What kind of weather do you like most?	**Больше всего мне нравится солнечная погода.** I like sunny weather most of all.
Какая сегодня погода? What is the weather like today?	**Сегодня солнечно.** It's sunny today. **Сегодня солнечная погода.** The weather is sunny today.
Какая погода была вчера? What was the weather like yesterday?	**Вчера было прохладно.** It was cool yesterday. **Погода вчера была прохладная.** The weather was cool yesterday.
Какая погода будет завтра? What will the weather be like tomorrow?	**Завтра будет туманно.** It will be foggy tomorrow. **Завтра будет туманная погода.** The weather will be foggy tomorrow.
Ты знаешь прогноз погоды на завтра? Do you know the weather forecast for tomorrow?	**Да, прогноз говорит, что будет холодно и ветрено.** Yes, the forecast says it will be cold and windy.
Какой прогноз погоды на завтра? What is the weather forecast for tomorrow?	**Плюс два днём и минус пять ночью.** Plus two in the afternoon and minus five at night.

📑 EXERCISES

01. Match the images with the descriptions of weather.

( ) **1)**	**A)** На улице сегодня идёт снег.
( ) **2)** +33 °C	**B)** Погода сегодня ветреная/на улице ветрено.
( ) **3)**	**C)** Сегодня жара/на улице очень жарко.
( ) **4)**	**D)** Сегодня туманная погода/на улице туманно.
( ) **5)**	**E)** На улице мороз/сегодня морозно. Сегодня морозный день.

( ) 6)	-27 °C	**F)** Сегодня идёт дождь.
( ) 7)		**G)** На улице облачно/сегодня облачный день.
( ) 8)	-9 °C	**H)** Сегодня тепло/тёплая погода. Сегодня тёплый день.
( ) 9)		**I)** Сегодня солнечная погода/на улице солнечно.
( ) 10)	+15 °C	**J)** На улице холодно. Сегодня холодная погода.

02. Go back to Exercise 1 and say what the weather was like yesterday / what it will be like tomorrow. Use the patterns below to make the sentences and to check their correctness.

Example:

Вчера было холодно. – It was cold yesterday. – было + adverb

Погода (день) вчера была (был) холодная (ый). – The weather (day) was cold yesterday. – Noun + была/был + adjective

Завтра будет холодно/холодный день. – It'll be cold/a cold day tomorrow.

Шёл дождь/будет идти дождь. – It was raining/it will rain.

_____

_____

_____

_____

_____

_____

_____

_____

_____

_____.

03. Read the sentences about the weather and underline the correct option.

1) Завтра будет **солнечная/солнечный** день.

2) Вчера **идёт/шёл** град.

3) Сегодня прохладная **день/погода**.

4) Завтра **будет/был** туман.

5) Завтра **шёл/будет** идти снег.

6) Вчера **была/было** очень холодно.

7) Сегодня мороз – **минус/плюс** двадцать пять градусов!

8) Сегодня **идёт/шёл** дождь.

9) Завтра будет **душная/душно**.

10) Вчера была **морозная/морозный** погода.

04. Listen to the descriptions of weather and match them with the images below.

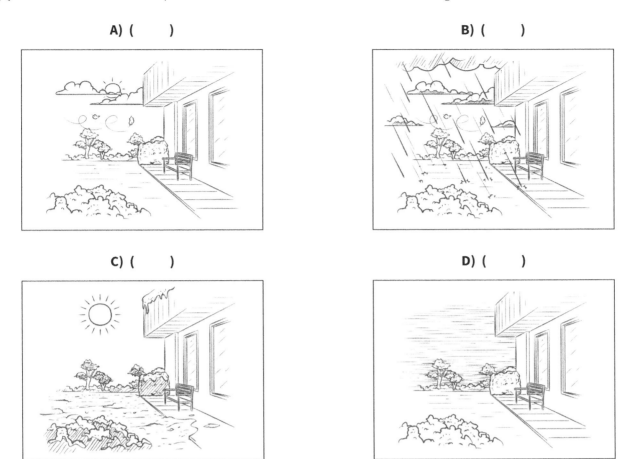

A) (   )

B) (   )

C) (   )

D) (   )

05. Match the questions with the answers.

( ) **1)** Какая погода тебе нравится больше всего?	**A)** Нет, мне больше всего нравится прохладная погода.
( ) **2)** Какая погода будет завтра?	**B)** Холодно? Прохладно - да! Но не холодно.
( ) **3)** Тебе нравится жаркая погода?	**C)** Больше всего мне нравится тёплая погода – я не люблю жару и мороз.
( ) **4)** Завтра будет идти снег?	**D)** Мне не нравится ветреная погода.
( ) **5)** Минус десять градусов – это холодно?	**E)** О, да! А потом шёл град!
( ) **6)** Ты знаешь прогноз погоды на завтра?	**F)** Завтра будет душно.
( ) **7)** Какая погода тебе не нравится?	**G)** Нет, а ты?
( ) **8)** Дождь вчера был сильный?	**H)** Нет, завтра не будет снега.

06. Answer the questions from Exercise 5 yourself and ask your partner.

UNIT V
BUYING, ORDERING, AND PAYING

This unit includes vocabulary and grammar constructions you'll need when shopping for clothes, food, and other essentials, as well as when eating out or ordering things. For the sake of convenience, logic, and more efficient remembering, this unit is divided into two parts.

PART I - SHOPPING
VOCABULARY

As usual, read the text, comparing its Russian and English parts to start building your vocabulary on the topic.

📢 Покупки - Shopping

Я люблю **ходить за покупками**. Мне нравится покупать **одежду** и **обувь**. Обычно я покупаю их **в торговом центре** или **универмаге**. У меня есть любимые **продавцы**. Они могут помочь мне **выбрать размер** и **цвет**.

I like to **go shopping**. I like buying **clothes** and **shoes**. I usually buy them **at a mall** or **a department store**. I have my favorite **shop assistants**. They can help me choose the **size** and the **color**.

Мне также нравится **покупать онлайн**, но есть один недостаток – нельзя **примерить** одежду. Иногда я **заказываю игрушки** для детей онлайн. Это **недорого** и удобно.

I also like **buying online** but there is one drawback – you can't **try** clothes **on**. Sometimes I **order** children's **toys** online. It's **inexpensive** and convenient.

Но я не люблю покупать **продукты**. **Молоко**, **хлеб**, **мясо**, **овощи** – это скучно! Я захожу в **супермаркет**, кладу всё в **тележку**, **плачу картой**, и ухожу домой. А вам нравится ходить за покупками?

But I don't like shopping for **groceries**. **Milk**, **bread**, **meat**, **vegetables** – that's boring! I enter the **supermarket**, put everything in the **cart**, **pay with a card** and go home. And do you like shopping?

📢 PLACES TO SHOP AT

For each noun there is a form in the prepositional case with a preposition. This form is useful when saying where you can buy something.

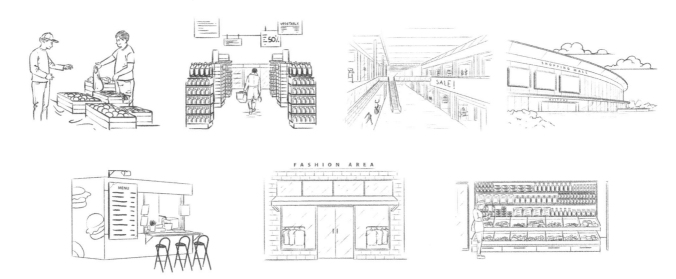

рынок на рынке	market
супермаркет в супермаркете	supermarket
универмаг в универмаге	department store
торговый центр в торговом центре	shopping mall
ларёк в ларьке	stall, stand
магазин одежды в магазине одежды	clothes' shop
продуктовый магазин в продуктовом магазине	grocery store

📢 MONEY AND PAYMENT

деньги	money
монета/ы	coin/s
копейка*/и	kopeck/s
наличные	cash
сдача/давать сдачу	change/give change
без сдачи	exact change
карта/карточка (Russian people use the second, diminutive form more often)	payment card
чек	check
платить (за что-то) наличными /картой/карточкой/чеком	pay (for something) in cash/with card/by check
(не)дорогой	(in)expensive
дешёвый	cheap
стоить	to cost

💡 *In Russian currency, kopeck is an equivalent for penny/cent. Very often the word denotes small change or is used to indicate that something is really inexpensive.

Example: С вас триста рублей, **двадцать копеек**. – It'll cost you three hundred rubles and **twenty kopecks**.

У тебя есть **копейки**? Я хочу дать немного нищему у входа. – Do you have **small change**? I want to give some to the beggar at the entrance.

Это платье стоило шестьсот рублей? **Копейки**! – This dress cost six hundred rubles? **Next to nothing**!

ПЛАТИТЬ, ЗАПЛАТИТЬ, AND ОПЛАТИТЬ

All these verbs are translated into English as 'to pay'. Here is how they differ:

Платить

- Habitual or current actions in the present;

Сегодня в кафе **плачу** я. – Today I'm paying at the café.
Обычно мы **платим** за электричество в конце месяца. – We usually pay electricity bills at the end of the month.

- Habitual actions in the past;

Он всегда **платил** за квартиру вовремя. – He always **paid** the rent on time.

-Used with the preposition 'за' it is the Russian equivalent to 'to pay for'.

Я не хочу **платить за** эти фрукты. Они несвежие! – I don't want to **pay for** this fruit. It's not fresh.

Заплатить

- Not used in the present form;

- Single, not repeated action in the past or in the future;

Я **заплатила** за доставку вчера. – I **paid** for the delivery yesterday.
Мы **заплатим** за заказ завтра. – We will pay for the order tomorrow.

- Used in the infinitive after the verbs like 'хотеть – want', 'мочь – can', 'нужно – need' to define one-time actions;

Мне **нужно заплатить** за горячую воду. – I **need to pay** the hot water bill.
Она не **может заплатить** за это дорогое пальто. – She **can't pay** for this expensive coat.

- Also used with the preposition 'за'.

Ты можешь **заплатить за** обед сегодня? – Can you **pay for** the lunch today?

Оплатить

- Is never followed by a preposition;

Могу я **оплатить** продукты картой? – Can I **pay** for the groceries with a card?

- Should always be followed by a noun (unlike the previous two words).

Вы можете **оплатить покупки** онлайн. – You can **pay for the purchases** online.
Вы можете **заплатить** онлайн. – You can **pay** online.

📢 OTHER USEFUL WORDS AND EXPRESSIONS

касса идти на кассу на кассе	checkout to go to the checkout at the checkout
покупки	bought items, purchases (all the things you've bought) Твои покупки такие тяжёлые! – Your purchases are so heavy!
очередь	queue/line
кассир	cashier
продавец	seller/shop assistant
покупатель	buyer
цена	price
тележка	shopping cart
пакет	shopping bag (plastic one)
купить/покупать*	buy
идти/ходить за покупками**	go shopping
скидка/и купить по скидке товар на скидке	discount/s buy at a discount discounted product
распродажа купить на распродаже	sale buy at a sale

* The difference between the verbs 'купить' and 'покупать' is similar to that between 'идти' and 'ходить' (see page 101).

'Купить' refers to a one-time action and is used either in the infinitive or in the past form.

Example:

Я хочу **купить** новые кроссовки. – I want **to buy** new sneakers.
Она **купила** продукты к ужину. – She **bought** groceries for dinner.

'Покупать' refers either to a repeated action or to an action in present.

Example:

Моя бабушка **покупает** овощи только на рынке. – My grandmother **buys** vegetables only at the marketplace.

Я сейчас **покупаю** продукты в магазине. Тебе что-нибудь нужно? – **I'm buying** groceries at the shop now. Do you need anything?

📢 SHOPPING FOR FOOD

еда	food
продукты	groceries
напитки	drinks/beverages
свежий	fresh
хлеб буханка хлеба белый/чёрный хлеб	bread loaf of bread white/rye bread
батон	kind of white bread
соль	salt
сахар	sugar
мясо курица/свинина/говядина	meat chicken/pork/beef
колбаса	salami/cooked sausage
сосиски	sausage
рыба	fish
молоко	milk
сметана	sour cream
кефир	kefir

йогурт	yogurt
майонез	mayonnaise
сыр	cheese
творог	cottage cheese
сливки	cream
сливочное масло	butter
растительное масло	oil
овощ/овощи	vegetable/s
фрукт/ы	fruit/s
макароны	pasta
рис	rice
гречка	buckwheat
минеральная вода	mineral water
сок	juice
чай	tea
кофе	coffee
пиво	beer
конфеты	sweets/candies
жевательная резинка	chewing gum

 The words in bold indicate food that is really popular in Russian cuisine and can sometimes cause confusion for foreign speakers. Take a look at the images to get a better understanding of what it looks like.

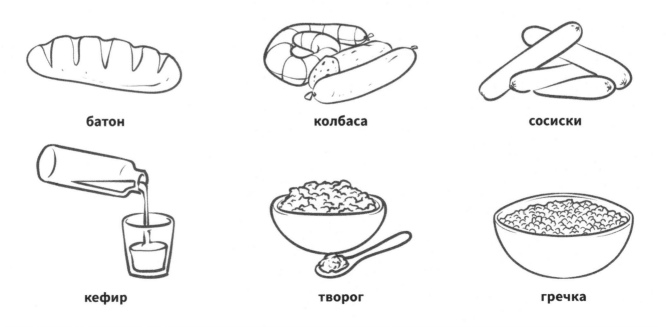

батон　　　　**колбаса**　　　　**сосиски**

кефир　　　　**творог**　　　　**гречка**

🔊 FRUITS AND VEGETABLES

банан/ы	banana/s
апельсин/ы	orange/s
мандарин/ы	mandarin/s
яблоко/и	apple/s
груша/и	pear/s
ананас/ы	pineapple/s
лимон/ы	lemon/s
виноград	grapes
персик/и	peach/es
картофель (more often colloquially called 'картошка')	potatoes
помидор/ы	tomato/s
огурец/огурцы	cucumber/s
перец	pepper
салат	lettuce
морковь	carrots
лук	onions

UNITS OF MEASUREMENT*

килограмм**	kilo
грамм	gram
литр	liter

*The things measured follow the unit and are used in the genitive case. If a word can be used in plural, then it will be genitive plural.

Example:

Два **килограмма помидоров**, пожалуйста. – Two **kilos of tomatoes**, please.

Триста **грамм колбасы**, пожалуйста. – Three hundred **grams of sausage**, please.

 **The units of measure can take different forms depending on the numeral that precedes them.

килограмм, грамм	1, 5-10, and numerals ending in these numbers
килограмм**а**, грамм**а**	2, 3, 4, and numerals ending in these numbers (except 12 -14)
литр	1
литра	2-4 and numerals ending in these numbers (except 12 -14)
литров	the rest of numerals

🔊 SHOPPING FOR CLOTHES AND SHOES

одежда	clothes
обувь	shoes
размер	size
большой/маленький	big/small
узкий/широкий	narrow/wide
длинный/короткий	long/short
примерочная	dressing room/changing room
примерить + accusative	try on
брюки	trousers
штаны	pants
джинсы	jeans
рубашка	shirt
футболка	T-shirt
нижнее бельё	underwear
костюм	suit
свитер	sweater
юбка	skirt
платье	dress
куртка	jacket
пальто	coat
шуба	fur coat
шапка	hat
ботинки	shoes (usually for colder seasons)
кроссовки	sneakers
сапоги	boots
туфли	shoes (elegant, for warmer seasons)

🔊 SHOPPING FOR OTHER THINGS

лекарства/таблетки	drugs/pills
ручка/и	pen/s
карандаш/и	pencil/s
конверт/ы	envelope/s
марка/и	stamp/s
стиральный порошок	laundry detergent
шампунь	shampoo
гель для душа	shower gel
игрушка/и	toy/s
сувенир	souvenir/keepsake

📢 COMMON CONVERSATIONAL FORMULAS

Я ищу + accusative	I'm looking for…
Мне нужно + accusative	I need…
Я бы хотел/а …	I would like to …
Где я могу найти + accusative?	Where can I find…?
У вас есть + accusative?	Do you have…?
Дайте мне, пожалуйста + accusative	Give me …, please.
У вас есть размер больше/меньше?	Do you have a bigger/smaller size?
У вас есть это в другом цвете?	Do you have it in a different color?
Где я могу примерить это?	Where can I try it on?
Это слишком дорого!	It's too expensive!
Спасибо, но это мне не подходит.	Thanks, but it doesn't suit me (both about clothes and general conditions).
Дайте мне, пожалуйста + accusative	Could you please give me …?
Сколько это стоит?	How much does it cost?
Сколько за килограмм/штуку?	How much per kilo/piece?
Я беру эту* шляпу.	I'll take this hat.
Я могу расплатиться картой?	Can I pay by card?
Какой у вас размер одежды/обуви?	What is your (clothing/shoe) size?
Как вы будете платить?	How are you going to pay?
Наличные или карта?	Cash or card?
С вас сто рублей.	It'll cost you a hundred rubles.
Вот, пожалуйста.	Here you are.
Что-нибудь ещё?	Anything else?
Во сколько вы открываетесь/закрываетесь?	When do you open/close? (Can be applied to ask about shop's/café's/cinema's, etc. working hours).

* 'Эту' is a form of demonstrative pronoun that is the Russian for 'this'. See the Grammar Appendix (pages 189-190) for more information on demonstrative pronouns as they are widely used in the context of buying things.

HOW TO SAY YOU WANT SOMETHING?

Subject + хотеть* in the present form + infinitive

Она хочет купить подарки для семьи.

She wants to buy presents for her family.

Subject + бы хотеть** in the past form + infinitive

(more polite)

Я бы хотела продать свою машину.

I would like to sell my car.

Subject in dative + нужно + infinitive + noun in accusative

Ему нужно купить конверты для писем.

He needs to buy envelopes for letters.

*See the present form on pages 186-189

**See the rules for past forms on pages 106-107

📑 EXERCISES

01. Write the correct word under each image. First, rely on your memory and then refer to the vocabulary section.

1)

_____.

2)

_____.

3)

_____.

4)

_____.

5)

_____.

6)

_____.

7)

_____.

8)

_____.

9)

_____.

10)

_____.

02. Do the same as in Exercise 1.

1)

_____.

2)

_____.

3)

_____.

4)

_____.

5)

_____.

6)

_____.

7)

_____.

8)

_____.

9)

_____.

10)

_____.

03. Match the descriptions with the objects. The descriptions are in Russian, but they are really simple.

( ) **1)** Свитер	**A)** Популярная еда в Италии.
( ) **2)** Цена	**B)** Это фрукт. Он оранжевый.
( ) **3)** Макароны	**C)** Это овощ. Он может быть красным, жёлтым и зелёным.
( ) **4)** Лимон	**D)** Это обувь для спорта.
( ) **5)** Игрушка	**E)** Сколько стоит вещь.
( ) **6)** Перец	**F)** Это жёлтый фрукт.
( ) **7)** Апельсин	**G)** Это одежда для холодной погоды.
( ) **8)** Кроссовки	**H)** Это для детей.

04. Group these words into the columns and check your work with the answer key.

Нижнее бельё, свинина, салат, молоко, картофель, чай, ананас, рис, сапоги, платье, лук, курица, штаны, бананы, макароны, сосиски, ботинки, костюм, кефир, гречка, кофе, батон, персики, туфли, йогурт, колбаса, помидоры, мандарины, хлеб, сок, груши, сметана, говядина, морковь, сливки

Мясные продукты Meat products	Овощи Vegetables	Фрукты Fruits	Крупы и мука Grains and flour

Одежда Clothes	Обувь Shoes	Молочные продукты Dairy products	Напитки Beverages

05. Make questions and answers for the things listed below. Note that the noun denoting the thing you want to buy should be in the accusative case.

Example:

- Где я могу купить лекарства? – Where can I buy medicine?
- В аптеке. – In a drugstore.

1) Куртка

_____

_____

2) Стиральный порошок

_____

_____

3) Одежда

_____

_____

4) Сувениры

_____

_____

5) Продукты

_____

_____

6) Овощи и фрукты

_____

_____

06. Read these sentences and choose the correct option.

1) Мама купила эти туфли **по/на** скидке.

2) Мне нужно пять **килограмм/килограмма** яблок.

3) Давай встретимся в **продуктовом/торговом** центре.

4) Кассир **не дал/оплатил** мне сдачу.

5) Мы всё купили. Пойдём на **кассу/кассе**.

6) Купи мне три **литров/литра** сока, пожалуйста.

7) У тебя есть **копейки/деньги**? Я хочу заплатить без сдачи.

8) Дайте мне триста **грамм/грамма** конфет, пожалуйста.

9) Папа купил эти брюки **в/на** распродаже.

10) Я не покупаю овощи в **супермаркет/супермаркете**.

11) Они взяли жевательную резинку на **кассу/кассе**.

12) Вы можете заплатить без **сдача/сдачи**?

07. Choose the correct option to practice the words with the same translation, but different usage patterns.

1) Тебе нужно **купить/покупать** молоко?

2) Мне нужно оплатить **-/за** посылку (parcel).

3) Где ты **покупаешь/купила** одежду? Ты всегда очень стильная.

4) Я не могу **заплатить/оплатить** сегодня. Я могу сделать это завтра?

5) Мы много **платим/заплатили** за школу каждый месяц. Но это очень хорошая школа!

6) Вчера я **купила/покупаю** эту шубу на распродаже.

7) Вам нужно **заплатить/оплатить** новые книги.

8) Мои родители хотят **купить/покупать** машину.

9) Мы уже **оплатили/заплатили** за покупки. Пойдём домой!

10) Наш сосед не любит **купить/покупать** одежду в интернете.

08. Use the correct form of the demonstrative pronouns. Define the gender of the noun the pronoun refers to, then define the case, and finally, choose the form.

1) Мне не нравится (этот) _____масло. Оно горькое (bitter).

2) Мама, мы можем купить мне (тот) _____юбку? Пожалуйста!

3) Мы заплатили за (этот) _____продукты, но они не свежие!

4) Я не могу приготовить салат без (этот) _____овощей.

5) Тебе нравятся (тот) _____ботинки? Они странные.

6) Моя дочь говорит о (тот) _____торговом центре весь день!

7) Он не хочет покупать (этот) _____брюки. Они слишком дорогие.

8) Спасибо, но мне не нужен (этот) _____пакет.

9) Дайте мне (тот) _____огурцы, пожалуйста. Три килограмма.

10) Я хочу примерить (этот) _____шапку.

Fill in the conversations with the logically fitting words. Check your work with the audio and roleplay the conversations.

Conversation I

Покупатель: Добрый день! Не могли бы вы помочь мне?

Продавец: Добрый день! Да, конечно! Что вам нужно?

Покупатель: Я бы хотел **1)** _____ костюм.

Продавец: Хорошо. Какой у вас **2)** _____?

Покупатель: Сорок восьмой, но я не уверен.

Продавец: Ничего страшного. Этот костюм сорок восьмого размера.

Покупатель: Он красивый! Где я могу его **3)** _____?

Продавец: 4) _____ вон там.

Через 5 минут

Покупатель: К сожалению, этот **4)** _____ мне не подходит.

Продавец: Почему?

Покупатель: Брюки слишком узкие. У вас есть размер **5)** _____.

Продавец: Да, конечно. Вот, пожалуйста.

Через 5 минут.

Покупатель: Этот размер идеальный! Я **6)** _____ этот костюм! Сколько он **7)** _____?

Продавец: Двенадцать тысяч рублей.

Покупатель: Это совсем не дорого!

Продавец: Да, костюм на **8)** _____. Как вы будете платить? **9)** _____ или картой?

Покупатель: Картой.

Buyer: Good afternoon! Could you please help me?

Seller: Good afternoon! Yes, of course! What do you need?

Buyer: I'd like to buy a suit.

Seller: Okay. What is your size?

Buyer: Forty-eight, but I'm not sure.

Seller: That's okay. This suit is size forty-eight.

Buyer: It's beautiful! Where can I try it on?

Seller: The dressing room is over there.

5 minutes later

Buyer: Unfortunately, this suit doesn't fit me.

Seller: Why?

Buyer: The trousers are too narrow. Do you have a bigger size?

Seller: Yes, of course. Here you are.

5 minutes later

Buyer: This size is perfect! I'll take this suit! How much does it cost?

Seller: Twelve thousand rubles.

Buyer: That's not expensive at all!

Seller: No, it isn't, the suit is at a discount. How will you pay? In cash or by card?

Buyer: By card.

Conversation II

A: Привет, Марина!

B: Привет, Настя!

A: Куда ты идёшь?

B: Я иду за покупками. У мужа завтра день рождения, и у нас будет много гостей.

A: Что ты **1)** _____ купить?

B: Мне **2)** _____ купить свежие овощи, фрукты и мясо.

A: Там на углу отличный ларёк! Они продают хорошие **3)** _____!

B: Я знаю, но там **4)** _____. Очень много людей, а я спешу.

A: Тогда пойдём на рынок! Я с тобой.

Через 15 минут на рынке.

B: Здравствуйте! У вас **4)** _____ свежие помидоры?

C: Добрый день! Да, вот они.

B: Сколько **5)** _____ килограмм?

C: Пятьсот рублей.

B: Хорошо. Дайте мне два **6)** _____, пожалуйста.

C: Что-нибудь ещё?

B: Да, я бы **7)** _____ купить салат, персики, ананас и лук.

C: Вот, пожалуйста. С вас две тысячи рублей. Вам нужен пакет?

B: Нет, спасибо. У меня есть свой.

A: Hi, Marina!

B: Hi, Nastya!

A: Where are you going?

B: I am going shopping. It's my husband's birthday tomorrow and we'll have many guests.

A: What do you want to buy?

B: I need to buy fresh vegetables, fruit, and meat.

A: There is a great stall at the corner over there! They sell good groceries!

B: I know, but there is a queue there. Lots of people, and I'm in a hurry.

A: Let's go to the market then! I'm coming with you.

15 minutes later at the market.

B: Hello! Do you have fresh tomatoes?

C: Good afternoon! Yes, here they are.

B: How much per kilo?

C: Five hundred rubles.

B: Okay. Give me two kilos, please.

C: Anything else?

B: Yes, I'd like to buy some lettuce, peaches, a pineapple, and onions.

C: Here you are. It'll cost you two thousand rubles. Do you need a bag?

B: No, thanks. I've got mine.

PART II - EATING OUT
Vocabulary

📢 В ресторане с другом - At a restaurant with a friend

В прошлый вторник мы с другом **пошли в ресторан**. Он получил новую работу, и мы хотели отметить. Мы **забронировали столик** заранее. Это был недорогой, но очень хороший ресторан.

Last Tuesday my friend and I **went to a restaurant**. He got a new job and we wanted to celebrate. We **booked a table** in advance. It was inexpensive, but a very good restaurant.

Официантка принесла нам **меню**. Я выбрала **отбивную** и **салат**. Мой друг **вегетарианец**, и у него было специальное меню. Блюда были очень **вкусные**. Но мне не понравился **десерт**. Он был слишком **сладкий**.

The **waitress brought** us the **menu**. I chose **a chop** and a **salad**. My friend is a **vegetarian**, and he had a special menu. The dishes were very **delicious**. But I didn't like the **dessert**. It was too **sweet**.

📢 ESSENTIAL NOUNS AND VERBS

меню	menu
стол (when Russian people talk about a table at a restaurant or a café, they use the diminutive form – 'столик')	table
стул	chair
официант/ка	waiter/waitress
чаевые	tip
счёт	check
блюдо	dish
закуска	appetizer
осовное блюдо	main dish
десерт	dessert
вилка	fork
ложка	spoon
нож	knife
тарелка	plate
миска	bowl
заказ	order
доставка	delivery

🔊 USEFUL WORD COMBINATIONS

забронировать столик	to book a table
пойти в ресторан/кафе	to go to a restaurant/café
пригласить в ресторан	to invite to eat out
позвать официанта	to call a waiter
попросить меню	to ask for the menu
выбрать блюдо	to choose the dish
заказать/сделать заказ	to order/place an order
попросить счёт	to ask a bill
взять еду с собой	to get takeout
заказать еду на дом	to order in
оставить чаевые	to leave a tip
положить товар в корзину	to add to cart
оформить заказ	to place an order
платная/бесплатная доставка	paid/free delivery

🔊 ADJECTIVES AND ADVERBS

(не) вкусный/вкусно	(un)tasty – adjective/adverb
сладкий/солёный	sweet/salty
горячий/холодный	hot/cold
быстрый/медленный	quick/slow
варёный	boiled
тушёный	stewed
жареный	fried
запечённый	grilled

🔊 THINGS TO ORDER

яичница/омлет	fried eggs/omelet
картофель фри/пюре	French fries/mashed potato
отбивная	chop
котлета	cutlet
овощное рагу	vegetable stew
салат	salad
суп	soup
паста	pasta
лапша	noodles

Мы бы хотели забронировать столик на понедельник.	We'd like to book a table for Monday.
У вас есть свободные столики?	Do you have available tables?
Официант, можно вас?	Waiter, can I have your attention, please?
Принесите меню, пожалуйста.	Bring the menu, please.
Вы готовы сделать заказ?	Are you ready to order?
Что вы будете заказывать?	What are you going to order?
Я буду/возьму + dish name in accusative	I'll have/take …
Счёт, пожалуйста.	Bill, please.
Моя еда холодная.	My food is cold.
У вас можно заказ еду на вынос/взять еду с собой?	Do you have takeout?
У вас есть блюда для вегитарианцев/веганов?	Do you have vegetarian/vegan dishes?
У меня аллергия на арахис/рыбу.	I'm allergic to peanuts/fish.

HOW TO SUGGEST DOING SOMETHING

Давай + verb in the 1st person plural in the future tense*

(when addressing someone as 'ты'. For 'вы' use 'давайте')

Давай пойдём в ресторан! – **Let's go** to the restaurant!

Друзья, **давайте забронируем** столик на завтра! – Friends, **let's book**

a table for tomorrow!

THE FUTURE TENSE

The future tense in Russian has two forms – a simple and a compound one. The correct formation of the form depends on the type of verb – if it's an imperfective or perfective one. Since the major goal of this book is building vocabulary and promoting basic communication and understanding skills, we're not going to focus on these differences.

However, we'll provide you with the part of the rule you'll need to independently build some basic future tense sentences.

The verbs you'll work with are all perfective. Their future tense corresponds to the English simple future and past future perfect tenses.

Example: Мы **пойдём** в кино завтра. – We **will go** to the cinema tomorrow.

К вечеру она **закончит** проект. – She **will have finished** the project by the evening.

Building the form is really simple.

1) Find the verb in a dictionary. Initial forms are usually imperfective.

2) Find its perfective form that is usually given in the dictionary as well.

3) Conjugate this verb according to the present tense pattern.

In the exercises below, you'll be given only perfective forms, so the process will be even easier.

Example: Забронировать – book (perfective form of the verb 'бронировать')

Мы **забронируем** номер в отеле заранее. – We **will book** a hotel room in advance.
Я **забронирую** для нас столик на вечер. – I **will book** a table for us for the evening.

🔆 Note some irregular patterns:

1) 'т' turns into 'д' in the verb **'пойти – go'** (the perfective form of the verb 'идти')
Я пойду, ты пойдёшь, мы пойдём, вы пойдёте, он/она/оно пойдёт, они пойдут.

2) Letter 'о' added in the verb **'позвать - call'**.
Я позову, ты позовёшь, мы позовём, etc.

3) 1st person singular of the verb **'попросить - ask'** is 'попрошу', the rest are regular, for example 'мы попросим'.

4) 1st person singular of the verb **'оставить - leave'** is 'оставлю', the rest are regular, for example 'он оставит'.

📝 EXERCISES

01. Write the corresponding word under each image. Use these words to fill in the table and make word combinations.

———————————————— .　　———————————————— .　　———————————————— .

———————————————— .　　———————————————— .　　———————————————— .

попросить	
забронировать	
позвать	
оставить	
пойти	
попросить	

02. Find an odd word in each row.

1) стол, заказ, стул

2) нож, тарелка, вилка, котлета, ложка

3) основное блюдо, лапша, десерт, закуска

4) вкусный, солёный, медленный, горячий

5) отбивная, рагу, паста

03. Put the adjective in the correct form to describe the nouns.

1) (быстрый) официант _____.

2) (медленный) доставка _____.

3) (хороший) кафе _____.

4) (вкусный) яичница _____.

5) (солёный) суп _____.

6) (запечённый) овощи _____.

7) (сладкий) сырники _____.

8) (горячий) лапша _____.

9) (невкусный) пюре _____.

10) (жареный) мясо _____.

04. Complete these sentences with the correct future tense of the verbs.

1) Давай (оформить) заказ онлайн. Я не хочу идти в магазин. _____.

2) Сегодня выходной, и они (заказать) еду на дом. _____.

3) У меня завтра день рождения. Мы с друзьями (пойти) в ресторан. _____.

4) Они (купить) продукты к ужину. _____.

5) Давайте (пойти) на прогулку. _____.

6) Я (заказать) блины с икрой и сливочным маслом. _____.

7) Давайте (поиграть) в волейбол на выходных. _____.

8) Я не могу выбрать. Давайте (позвать) официанта. _____.

9) Они (забронировать) столик на субботу. _____.

10) Я (заплатить) за обед сегодня. _____.

05. Match the questions and the answers.

( ) **1)** Вы хотите есть здесь или возьмёте еду с собой?	**A)** Нет, мы не можем выбрать. Не могли бы вы помочь нам?
( ) **2)** Тебе нравится заказывать еду на дом?	**B)** Да, вот специальное меню.
( ) **3)** Вы готовы сделать заказ?	**C)** Нет, я люблю есть в кафе.
( ) **4)** У вас есть блюда для вегетарианцев?	**D)** Да, конечно!
( ) **5)** Что вы будете заказывать?	**E)** К сожалению, все столики забронированы.
( ) **6)** Моя еда холодная. Вы можете принести мне тёплый суп?	**F)** Мы возьмём еду с собой.
( ) **7)** У вас есть свободные столики?	**G)** Да, вот блюда для детей.
( ) **8)** У вас есть меню для детей?	**H)** Я буду омлет и запечённые овощи.

06. Arrange the conversations in the correct order. Check your work with the audio and roleplay them.

Conversation I

A: Отлично! Давай поедем на такси!

B: Нет! Погода тёплая и солнечная. Давай пойдём пешком.

A: Я не хочу готовить сегодня.

A: Но я не хочу оставаться дома!

B: Не проблема! Давай закажем еду на дом.

A: Хорошо.

B: Ладно, давай пойдём в кафе.

_____

_____

_____

_____

_____

_____.

A: I don't want to cook today.

B: No problem! Let's order in.

A: But I don't want to stay home!

B: Okay, let's go to the café.

A: Great! Let's go by taxi!

B: No! The weather is warm and sunny. Let's go on foot.

A: Okay.

Conversation II

B: Да, но у меня есть вопрос. Этот десерт с арахисом?

B: Да, чёрный кофе. Без молока и без сахара.

B: Хорошо! У меня аллергия на арахис. Тогда я буду этот десерт, пожалуйста.

A: Здравствуйте! Вы готовы сделать заказ?

A: Какой-нибудь напиток?

A: Нет, в нём нет арахиса.

_____

_____

_____

_____

_____

_____

A: Hello! Are you ready to order?

B: Yes, but I've got a question. Are there peanuts in this dessert?

A: No, it has no peanuts.

B: That's good! I'm allergic to peanuts. I'll have this dessert, please.

A: Anything to drink?

B: Yes, black coffee. No milk and no sugar.

Conversation III

A: Я буду пюре, котлеты и овощной салат. Официант, мы готовы сделать заказ.

C: Я не ем мясо. Официант, можно вас? У вас есть веганское меню?

B: Вот, пожалуйста.

Через 20 минут

B: Да. Вот оно.

A: Официант, принесите меню, пожалуйста.

A: Еда была очень вкусная и недорогая. Давай оставим чаевые.

C: Спасибо! О, у них есть борщ без мяса. Отлично. Я возьму его. А ты?

A: Что закажем?

A: Да, у них есть борщ. Но он с мясом.

B: Принесите счёт, пожалуйста.

B: Давай.

C: Я не знаю. У них есть борщ? Я хочу что-нибудь горячее.

_____

_____

_____

_____

_____

_____

_____

_____

_____

_____

_____

_____

_____ .

A: Waiter, could you bring the menu please?

B: Here you are.

A: What shall we order?

C: I don't know. Do they have borscht? I want something hot.

A: Yes, they have borscht. But it's made with meat.

C: I don't eat meat. Waiter, may I have your attention for a while? Do you have a vegan menu?

B: Yes, here it is.

C: Thank you! They have borscht without meat. Great. I'll take it. And what about you?

A: I'll have mashed potatoes, a cutlet, and a vegetable salad. Waiter, we're ready to order.

20 minutes later

B: Bring us the bill, please.

A: The food was very tasty and inexpensive. Let's leave a tip.

B: Let's do it.

07. Make similar conversations and roleplay them with your partner.

CONCLUSION

That was a breathtaking ride, wasn't it? We know that it was also a kind of seesaw with ups and downs, wins and losses, disappointments and inspiration. No matter how much of each there was, here you are at a completely new level of Russian and we're glad to have been part of it.

After working hard, you will now feel more confident in a Russian—speaking environment. It absolutely doesn't matter how many mistakes you've made and how many you will make. What matters is that you've bridged the gap between nothing and something, between some and more, and have a background to go further.

So, what's next? You can and actually should go on honing your skills and gaining new knowledge. With lots of resources for the purpose, including other Lingo Mastery tools, this book still has value to offer. Although much has been learned and the exercises have been completed, it's always a good idea to go back to the vocabulary and look at it with fresh eyes, to analyze it with a mind that is now packed with more understanding, which will subsequently help you understand and memorize things better.

We also encourage you to turn to this resource before travelling to a Russian-speaking country or communicating with someone online, because there are lots of useful sentences and expressions for standard situations that were included for you to take a shortcut from knowing a word to using it in context.

We hope this book, and the sense of achievement it gave you, will be a motivation for you to continue the journey and take your Russian to new heights as you improve and grow.

Good luck and we hope to see you in other books by Lingo Mastery!

GRAMMAR APPENDIX

GENDER OF NOUNS

There are three genders in Russian: **masculine, feminine, and neuter (neutral)**. Very often grammatical gender is attributed to the noun according to physical gender, like in 'мать' - 'mother', which is feminine.

With other nouns, especially inanimate ones, it's different. The good news is that you don't need to memorize the gender of each noun (like in German, for example). The gender can easily be defined by the ending of the noun in its initial form, with a few exceptions.

Masculine	Feminine	Neutral
The last letter of the word is a **consonant** or **'й'**.	The last letter is **'а'** or **'я'**.	The last letter is **'о'** or **'е'**.
For example: Певец – Singer Нищий – Beggar	**For example:** Профессия – Profession Книга – Book	**For example:** Окно – Window Море – Sea

Although the gender of most nouns can be defined by their endings, there is still some memorizing to do.

If a noun ends in **'ь'** (soft sign), it can be either masculine or feminine. Generally speaking, the gender of such nouns should be memorized, but it's still possible to form certain groups.

The following nouns that end in 'ь' are always masculine:

- Names of months (октябрь – October, июнь – June);
- Nouns that end with **'-арь'** (календарь – calendar);
- Nouns that end with **'-тель'** (учитель – teacher).

The following nouns that end in '-ь' are always feminine:

- Nouns that end with **'-чь'**, **'-шь'**, **'-щь'** (ночь – night).

Exceptions to the rule that occur due to physical gender:

Папа – Dad (masculine);

Дядя – Uncle (masculine);

Дедушка – Grandfather (masculine);

Мужчина – Man (masculine).

SINGULAR AND PLURAL FORMS OF NOUNS

Gender	Ending Changes	Examples
Masculine	Consonant – cons. + 'ы'*	велосипе**д** – велосипе**ды** bike – bikes
	'й' turns into 'и'	музе**й** – музе**и** museum – museums
	'ь' turns into 'и'	шампун**ь** – шампун**и** shampoo – shampoos
Feminine	'а' turns into 'ы'**	мам**а** – мам**ы** mom – moms
	'я' turns into 'и'	недел**я** – недел**и** week – weeks
	'ия' turns into 'ии'	коллекц**ия** – коллекц**ии** collection – collections
	'ь' turns into 'и'	ноч**ь** – ноч**и** night – nights
Neutral	'о' turns into 'а'	окн**о** – окн**а** window - windows
	'е' turns into 'я'	мор**е** – мор**я** sea – seas
	'ие' turns into 'ия'	желан**ие** – желан**ия** wish – wishes
	'мя' turns into 'ена'	им**я** – имен**а** name – names

*There are exceptions to this rule. The following words take '**а/я' instead of 'ы'**:

доктор (doctor) – доктора
адрес (address) – адреса
вечер (evening) – вечера
глаз (eye) – глаза
город (city) – города
паспорт (passport) – паспорта
поезд (train) – поезда
учитель (teacher) – учителя

If the ending is preceded by **к, х, ж, ч, г, ш, or щ, the plural form is created with the ending '**и' instead of 'ы'**.

Example: Мальчик – мальчики (boy – boys)
         Книга – книги (book – books)

NOUNS THAT ARE ALWAYS PLURAL

Деньги – Money

Брюки – Trousers

Штаны – Pants

Ботинки – Shoes

Носки – Socks

Часы – Watches, clock

Ножницы – Scissors

Духи – Perfume

Каникулы – Holidays

Шахматы – Chess

Очки – Glasses

Ворота – Gates

NOUNS THAT ARE ALWAYS SINGULAR

1) Uncountable substances, for example, вода (water), свет (light), молоко (milk).

2) Abstract notions, feelings and emotions, for example, любовь (love), радость (joy), грусть (sadness).

3) Collective nouns like мебель (furniture), посуда (cutlery), обувь (footwear).

Note that sometimes the native language can trick you. For example, 'hair' in English is always singular (unless we mean separate hairs), while in Russian 'волосы' is plural.

'Police' is always plural in English, while in Russian 'полиция' is always singular.

NOUNS THAT COINCIDE IN SINGULAR AND PLURAL

метро (subway) – метро

пианино (piano) – пианино

кофе (coffee) – кофе

хобби (hobby) – хобби

пальто (coat) – пальто

радио (radio) – радио

шоссе (highway) – шоссе

меню (menu) – меню

IRREGULAR PLURALS

мать (mother) – матери

дочь (daughter) – дочери

ребёнок (child) – дети

цветок (flower) – цветы

яблоко (apple) – яблоки

NOUNS THAT TAKE THE ENDING '-ья'

дерево (tree) – деревья

брат (brother) – братья

друг (friend) – друзья

сын (son) – сыновья

крыло (wing) – крылья

лист (leaf) – листья

стул (chair) – стулья

CASES OF PERSONAL PRONOUNS

Nominative	Genitive	Dative	Accusative	Instr.	Prepositional
Я – I	Меня	Мне	Меня	Мной	Мне
Ты – You	Тебя	Тебе	Тебя	Тобой	Тебе
Мы – We	Нас	Нам	Нас	Нами	Нас
Вы – You	Вас	Вам	Вас	Вами	Вас
Он – He	Его	Ему	Его	Им	Нём
Она – She	Её	Ей	Её	Ею	Ней
Оно – It	Его	Ему	Его	Им	Нём
Они – They	Их	Им	Их	Ими	Них

POSSESSIVE PRONOUNS, THEIR GENDER, NUMBER, AND CASES

Gender Number	Nominative	Genitive	Dative	Accusative Anim.	Accusative Inanim.	Instrumental	Prepositional
Masculine Singular	Мой	Мо**его**	Мо**ему**	Мо**его**	Мой	Мо**им**	Мо**ём**
	Твой	Тво**его**	Тво**ему**	Тво**его**	Твой	Тво**им**	Тво**ём**
	Наш	Наш**его**	Наш**ему**	Наш**его**	Наш	Наш**им**	Наш**ем**
	Ваш	Ваш**его**	Ваш**ему**	Ваш**его**	Ваш	Ваш**им**	Ваш**ем**
Feminine Singular	Моя	Мо**ей**	Мо**ей**	Мо**ей**		Мо**ей**	Мо**ей**
	Твоя	Тво**ей**	Тво**ей**	Тво**ю**		Тво**ей**	Тво**ей**
	Наша	Наш**ей**	Наш**ей**	Наш**у**		Наш**ей**	Наш**ей**
	Ваша	Ваш**ей**	Ваш**ей**	Ваш**у**		Ваш**ей**	Ваш**ей**
Neutral Singular	Моё	Мо**его**	Мо**ему**	Мо**ё**		Мо**им**	Мо**ём**
	Твоё	Тво**его**	Тво**ему**	Тво**ё**		Тво**им**	Тво**ём**
	Наше	Наш**его**	Наш**ему**	Наш**е**		Наш**им**	Мо**ём**
	Ваше	Ваш**его**	Ваш**ему**	Ваш**е**		Ваш**им**	Ваш**ем**
Plural	Мои	Мо**их**	Мо**им**	Мо**их**	Мои	Мо**ими**	Мо**их**
	Твои	Тво**их**	Тво**им**	Тво**их**	Твои	Тво**ими**	Тво**их**
	Наши	Наш**их**	Наш**им**	Наш**их**	Наши	Наш**ими**	Наш**их**
	Ваши	Ваш**их**	Ваш**им**	Ваш**их**	Ваши	Ваш**ими**	Ваш**их**

Note that possessive pronouns 'его', 'её', and 'их' are the same for all genders, numbers, and cases, so they are not included in the table.

Example:

Я знаю **её** маму. – I know her mother. (feminine, accusative)

Я помогаю **её** маме. – I help her mother. (feminine, dative)

Я пришла без **её** брата. – I came without her brother. (masculine, genitive)

Я думаю о **её** брате. – I'm thinking about her brother. (masculine, prepositional)

The above table can be rather discouraging, but pay attention to the fact that many forms coincide:

1) Masculine genitive singular = masculine accusative singular animate.

2) All cases except the nominative in feminine are the same.

3) Neutral singular in genitive, dative, instrumental, and prepositional are the same as in masculine singular.

4) Genitive plural = accusative plural animate.

DECLENSION OF THE PRONOUN 'СВОЙ' ACCORDING TO NUMBER, GENDER, AND CASE

Gender/number	Nominative	Genitive	Dative	Accusative	Instr.	Prepositional
Masculine	Свой	Своего	Своему	Своего	Своим	Своём
Feminine	Своя	Своей	Своей	Свою	Своей	Своей
Neutral	Своё	Своего	Своему	Своё	Своим	Своём
Plural	Свои	Своих	Своим	Своих	своими	Своих

CASES OF NOUNS

There are six cases in the Russian language. All of them make nouns change their endings accordingly.

Именительный падеж - Nominative case

Indicates: The subject of the sentence.

Notes: All the nouns in Russian dictionaries are in the nominative case. So, the only change that can occur is when a noun takes a plural form.

Example:

Мой брат часто опаздывает на работу.
My brother is often late for work. (Кто – who?)

Мой дом далеко от офиса.
My house is far away from the office. (Что – what?)

РОДИТЕЛЬНЫЙ ПАДЕЖ – GENITIVE CASE

Indicates: Possession, attribution or absence

Gender	Ending Changes	Examples
Masculine	Consonant – cons. + 'a'	Велосипе**д** – Bike У меня нет велосипед**а**. I don't have a bike.
	'й' turns into 'я'	Хокк**ей** – Hockey Я не фанат хокке**я**. I am not a hockey fan.
	'ь' turns into 'я'	Коктейл**ь** – Cocktail Хочешь клубничного коктейл**я**? Would you like some strawberry cocktail?
Feminine	'a' turns into 'ы'*	Мам**а** – Mom Ты пришёл без мам**ы**? Have you come without your mom?
	я' turns into 'и'	Тёт**я** – Aunt Это дом моей тёт**и**. This is my aunt's house.
	'ия' turns into 'ии'	Полиц**ия** – Police Здесь нет полиц**ии**. There are no police here.
	'ь' turns into 'и'	Обув**ь** – Shoes У неё нет зимней обув**и**. She doesn't have winter shoes.
Neutral	'o' turns into 'a'	Окн**о** – Window Я вижу тебя из окн**а**. I can see you from the window.
	'e' turns into 'я'	Мор**е** – Sea Это фотография мор**я**. This is a photo of the sea.
	'мя' turns into 'мени'	И**мя** – Name У моего щенка ещё нет **имени**. My puppy doesn't have a name yet.
	'ие' turns into 'ия'	Желан**ие** – Wish У меня нет желан**ия** идти на прогулку. I don't have any wish to go for a walk.

* According to the spelling rules, consonants **г, к, х, ж, ч, ш,** and **щ** are never followed by the vowel 'ы', so feminine nouns that have these consonants before the ending take **'и'** instead of 'ы'.

Example: Книг**а** - Книг**и**

У меня нет это**й** книги. – I don't have this book.

Irregular genitive:

Мать – матери (Mother)
Дочь – дочери (Daughter)

Note that the nouns that end in **'a'** and **'я'**, but are masculine according to their physical gender (like папа, дедушка, дядя), form their endings like feminine nouns.

Я не хожу в школу без пап**ы**. – I don't go to school without my dad.

THE PLURAL OF THE GENITIVE CASE

Gender	Ending Changes	Examples
Masculine	Consonant – cons. + 'ов'*	Вопро**с** – Question У меня много вопрос**ов**. I've got a lot of questions.
	'й' turns into 'ев'	Геро**й** – Hero Сейчас нет героев. There are no heroes nowadays.
	'ь' turns into 'ей'	Учител**ь** – Teacher У нас в школе мало учител**ей**. We've got few teachers at our school.
Feminine	the ending 'a' is removed**	Племянниц**а** – Niece Почему ты пришла без своих племянниц? Why have you come without your nieces?
	'я' turns into 'ь'	Нян**я** – Babysitter В агенстве нет свободных нян**ь**. They don't have available babysitters at the agency.
	'ия turns into ий	Виктор**ия** – Victoria (female name) У нас в офисе нет Виктор**ий**. Вы ошиблись. We don't have Victorias at our office. You're mistaken.
	'ь' turns into 'ей'	Бол**ь** – Pain (can be plural in Russian) У меня больше нет бол**ей** в спине. I don't have any pain in my back anymore.
	the ending 'o' is removed	Лиц**о** – Face Здесь так много знакомых **лиц**! There are so many familiar faces here!
	'е' turns into 'ей'	Мор**е** – Sea В нашей стране нет мор**ей**. There are no seas in our country.
Neutral	'мя' turns into 'мён'	И**мя** – Name Я не могу запомнить столько и**мён**. I can't remember so many names.
	'ие' turns into 'ий'	Желан**ие** – Wish Ты загадал так много желан**ий**! You made so many wishes!

*If a masculine noun ends in **ж, ч, ш** or **щ,** it takes the ending **'ей'** instead of **'ов'.**

Example: Му**ж** – нет муж**ей** (Husband – no husbands)

Вра**ч** – нет врач**ей** (Doctor – no doctors)

** If the noun ends in a consonant cluster after the ending is removed, place 'е/о' between these consonants.

For example: Деву**шк**а – много девуш**е**к (Girlfriend – many girlfriends).

Irregular forms of genitive plural:

Братья (brothers) – братьев

Друзья (friends) – друзей

Сыновья (sons) – сыновей

Англичанин (Englishman) – англичан

Дочери (daughters) – дочерей

Матери (mothers) – матерей

Дети (children) – детей

Люди (people) – людей

ДАТЕЛЬНЫЙ ПАДЕЖ – DATIVE CASE

Indicates: That something is given or addressed to the person or object.

Notes: 'Дать' is the Russian word for 'give', which makes it easier to memorize the case name.

Gender	Ending Changes	Examples
Masculine	Consonant – cons. + 'у'	Бра**т** – Brother Я купил брат**у** новую книгу. I've bought a new book for my brother.
	'й' turns into 'ю'	Гер**ой** – Hero Он помог гер**ою**. He has helped the hero.
	'ь' turns into 'ю'	Строител**ь** – Builder Мы отдали материалы строител**ю**. We gave the materials to the builder.
Feminine	'а' turns into 'е'	Сестр**а** – Sister Я подарю сестр**е** это платье. I will give this dress as a present to my sister.
	'я' turns into 'е'	Тёт**я** – Aunt Удели внимание тёт**е**, пожалуйста. Pay some attention to your aunt please.
	'ия' turns into 'ии'	Мар**ия** – Maria (Russian name) Это письмо отправили Мар**ии**. This letter has been sent to Maria.
	'ь' turns into 'и'	Ноч**ь** – Night Я рассказываю свои секреты только ноч**и**. I only share my secrets with the night.

Neutral	'o' turns into 'a'	Лиц**о** – Face Приложи лёд к лиц**у**. Put some ice on your face.
	'e' turns into 'ю'	Мор**е** – Sea Мор**ю** не нужен наш мусор! The sea doesn't need our trash!
	'мя' turns into 'мени'	Вре**мя** – Time Дай вре**мени** шанс. Всё будет хорошо. Give time a chance. Everything will be fine.

Irregular dative: Мать – дать что-то мат**ери** (Mother – give something to mother)

Дочь – дать что-то доч**ери** (Daughter – give something to daughter)

THE PLURAL OF THE DATIVE CASE

Gender	Ending Changes	Example
Masculine Feminine Neutral	Consonant + 'ам'	Вра**г** – Enemy Мы не отдадим золото враг**ам**! We won't give up the gold to our enemies!
	'а' turns into 'ам'	Дедушк**а** – Grandfather Мы купим нашим дедушк**ам** конфеты. We'll buy sweets for our grandfathers.
	'o' turns into 'ам'	Письм**о** – Letter Удели немного времени письм**ам**! Devote some time to letters!
	'й' turns into 'ам'/'ям'	Геро**й** – Hero Дети подарили геро**ям** цветы. Kids gave flowers to heroes.
	'ь' turns into 'ам'/'ям'	Пекар**ь** – Baker Мы привезли муку пекар**ям**. We've brought flour to the bakers.
	'e' turns into 'ям'	Мор**е** – Sea Он отдал свою жизнь мор**ям**. He gave his life to the seas.
	'я' turns into 'ам'/ям'	Дяд**я** – Uncle Мы показали дяд**ям** новый фильм. We showed our uncles a new movie.

Note that dative plural forms don't depend on the gender of the noun. Instead, they depend on the ending of the noun in nominative singular.

Irregular dative plural forms:

Братья (brothers) – братьям
Друзья (friends) – друзьям
Сыновья (sons) – сыновьям
Дочери (daughters) – дочерям
Матери (mothers) – матерям
Дети (children) – детям
Люди (people) – людям

Винительный падеж – Accusative case

Indicates: The object of the sentence, and is equivalent to the English objective case (him, them).

Many forms of the accusative case coincide with the previously studied forms and take minimal memorizing of new endings. For easy and correct formation of the accusative case forms, we must divide the nouns into two groups: animate and inanimate objects.

ACCUSATIVE CASE FOR ANIMATE OBJECTS

Animate objects are living beings, including people and animals.

Animate nouns singular	Animate nouns plural
Masculine **accusative = genitive** Это стол нашего врач**а**. (genitive) This is our doctor's table. Я вижу нашего врач**а**. (accusative) I see our doctor.	**Masculine** **accusative = genitive** Смотри на этих попуга**ев**! Какие милые! Look at these parrots! How cute they are!
Feminine Nouns that end with '**ь**' = nominative Мы уважаем Вашу доч**ь**. We respect your daughter. **'а' is replaced with 'у'** **'я' is replaced with 'ю'** Я помню твою подруг**у**/тёт**ю**. I remember your friend/aunt.	**Feminine** **accusative = genitive** Я не люблю кош**е**к. Я предпочитаю собак. I don't like cats. I prefer dogs.
Neutral animate nouns barely exist in the Russian language.	

ACCUSATIVE CASE FOR INANIMATE NOUNS

Inanimate nouns singular	Inanimate nouns plural
Masculine **accusative = nominative** **Пульт** лежит на столе. (nominative) **The remote control** is on the table. Я вижу **пульт**. (accusative) I see the **remote control**.	**accusative = nominative plural** **for all genders** Эти красные **цветы** красивые (nominative) These red **flowers** are beautiful. Мне нравятся эти **цветы**. (accusative) I like these **flowers**. **Моря** красивые. (nominative) **Seas** are beautiful. Я рисую моря. (accusative) I'm painting seas.
Feminine Nouns that end with **'ь'** = nominative Я обожаю ночь! Волшебное время! I love the night! It's a magical time! **'a' is replaced with 'у'** **'я' is replaced with 'ю'** Я читаю эту книг**у**. I'm reading this book. Я впервые вижу такую бур**ю**! It's the first time I see such a storm!	
Neutral **accusative = nominative** Окно грязное. (nominative) The window is dirty. Я мою окно. (accusative) I'm washing the window.	

Note that all exceptions, peculiarities, and irregular forms that belong to the genitive case, are applicable to the coinciding accusative forms.

Творительный падеж – Instrumental case

Indicates: What instrument is used to perform the action. With the help of whom or what, the action is completed. With whose participation the action is complete.

Gender	Ending Changes	Examples
Masculine	Consonant – cons. + 'ом'	Брат – Brother Я еду на экскурсию с брат**ом**. I'm going on an excursion with my brother.
	'й' turns into 'ем'	Геро**й** – Character Я интересуюсь геро**ем** этого рассказа. I'm interested in this story's character.
Feminine	'ь' turns into 'ем'	Строител**ь** – Builder Мой племянник работает строител**ем**. My nephew works as a builder.
	'а' turns into 'ой'	Сестр**а** – Sister Я горжусь своей сестр**ой**. I'm proud of my sister.
	'я' turns into 'ей'	Недел**я** - Week Я не доволен этой недел**ей**. I'm not happy with this week.
	'ь' + 'ю'	Ноч**ь** – Night Мы выезжаем ноч**ью**. We're leaving at night.
Neutral	'о' + 'м'	Лиц**о** – Face Что с твоим лиц**ом**? What is wrong with your face?
	'е' + 'м'	Солнц**е** – Sun Я наслаждаюсь солнц**ем**. I'm enjoying the sun.
	'мя' turns into 'менем'	Им**я** – Name Я горжусь своим и**менем**. I'm proud of my name.

Irregular instrumental:

Мать – матерью (Mother)
Дочь – дочерью (Daughter)

Note that according to the rules, vowels **ж, ч, ш,** and **щ** cannot be followed by an unstressed vowel **'о'.** In case it should be there according to the table, replace it with **'е'.**

Example:

Я иду на вечеринку вместе с муж**ем**. – I'm going to the party with my husband.

THE PLURAL OF THE INSTRUMENTAL CASE

Gender	Ending Changes	Examples
Masculine Feminine Neutral	Consonant + 'ами'	Сто**л** – Table Что вы делаете с этими стола**ми**? What are you doing with these tables?
	'a' turns into 'ами'	Бабушк**а** – Grandmother. Мы идём гулять с бабушка**ми**. We're going for a walk with our grandmothers.
	'o' turns into 'ам'	Письм**о** – Letter Займись этими письма**ми**! Их слишком много! Deal with these letters! There are too many of them!
	'й turns into 'ями'	Геро**й** – Hero Мы гордимся нашими геро**ями**. We're proud of our heroes.
	'ь' turns into 'ями'	Двер**ь** – Door Что за этими двер**ями**? What is behind these doors?
	'e' turns into 'ями'	Пол**е** – Field У него есть земли с большими пол**ями**. He's got lands with big fields.
	'я' turns into 'ями'	Нян**я** – Babysitter Нам не везёт с нян**ями**. We're not lucky with babysitters.

Note that instrumental plural forms don't depend on the gender of the noun. Instead, they depend on the ending of the noun in nominative singular.

Irregular instrumental plural:

Люди (people) – людьми

Предложный падеж – Prepositional case

Answers the questions: О ком? О чём? Где? – About whom? About what? Where?

Note: 'Предлог' is the Russian equivalent for 'preposition', which explains the name of the case, because it's often used with various prepositions, the most widespread of which are **'o' – 'about', 'на' – 'at' / 'on', 'в' – 'in'**. The latter two should be the prepositions of place, because when they indicate motion in some direction, the accusative case should be used instead:

Я иду **на** работ**у** (motion) – Я уже **на** работ**е** (place).
I'm going to work – I'm already at work.

Pay attention; the preposition 'o' can change into 'об' when it's followed by a vowel, and into 'обо' when it's followed by a consonant cluster, which is done for more convenient pronunciation.

Example:
Я не хочу думать **об э**том! – I don't want to think of it!
Вы говорите **обо мне?** – Are you talking about me?

Gender	Ending Changes	Examples
Masculine	Consonant – cons. + 'e'	Двоюродный бра**т** – Cousin Я думаю о моём двоюродном брат**е**. I'm thinking about my cousin.
Masculine	'й' turns into 'e'	Геро**й** – Character Она написала ессе об этом геро**е**. She's written an essay about this character.
Masculine	'ь' turns into 'e'	Водител**ь** – Driver Я ничего не знаю об этом водител**е**. I know nothing about this driver.
Feminine	'a' turns into 'e'	Мам**а** – Mom Мы говорим о нашей мам**е**. We're talking about our mom.
Feminine	'я' turns into 'e'	Недел**я** – Week Я не хочу даже думать об этой недел**е**! I don't even want to think about this week!
Feminine	'ь' turns into 'и'	Двер**ь** – Door Зонтик стоит у двер**и**. The umbrella is at the door.
Feminine	'ия' turns into 'ии'	Анастас**ия** – Anastasia Я не могу не думать об Анастас**ии**! I can't help thinking about Anastasia!
Neutral	'o' turns into 'e'	Лиц**о** – Face Все эмоции у тебя на лиц**е**! You've got all your emotions expressed on your face!
Neutral	'e' remains 'e'	Солнц**е** – The sun Я лежу на солнц**е**. I'm lying in the sun.
Neutral	'ие' turns into 'ии'	Здан**ие** – Building Все дети сейчас в здан**ии**. All the kids are in the building now.
Neutral	'мя' turns into 'мени'	Вре**мя** – Time Я думаю о свободном вре**мени** на этой неделе. I'm thinking about how to spend free time this week.

Irregular prepositional case:

Мать – матери (Mother)

Дочь – дочери (Daughter)

THE PLURAL OF THE PREPOSITIONAL CASE

Gender	Ending Changes	Examples
Masculine Feminine Neutral	Consonant + 'ах'	Мотоцик**л** – Motorcycle Поехали кататься на мотоцикл**ах!** Let's go ride motorcycles!
	'а' turns into 'ах'	Подруг**а** – Female friend. Мы говорим о наших подруг**ах**. We're talking about our friends.
	'о' turns into 'ах'	Лиц**о** – Face Я рада видеть счастье на ваших лиц**ах**! I'm glad to see happiness on your faces!
	'й' turns into 'ях'	Геро**й** – Hero Это книга о геро**ях** войны. This is a book about war heroes.
	'ь' turns into 'ях'	Звер**ь** – Beast '/ animal Это история о диких звер**ях**. This is a story about wild animals.
	'е' turns into 'ях'	Пол**е** – Field Цветы растут на пол**ях**. Flowers grow in the fields.
	'я' turns into 'ях'	Нян**я** – Babysitter Мамы разговаривают о нян**ях**. Moms are talking about babysitters.

Note that instrumental plural forms don't depend on the gender of the noun. Instead, they depend on the ending of the noun in nominative singular.

Irregular nouns in the plural prepositional case:

Братья (brothers) – братьях

Друзья (friends) – друзьях

Сыновья (sons) – сыновьях

Матери (mothers) – матерях

Дочери (daughters) – дочерях

Дети (children) – детях

Люди (people) – людях

RUSSIAN CASES, SUMMARY – SINGULAR

Case	Endings		
	Masculine	**Feminine**	**Neutral**
Nominative	Consonant, -й, -ь	-а, -я, -ь,	-о, -е, -мя
Genitive	-а, -я	-ы, -и	-а, -я, -мени
Dative	-у, -ю	-е, -ии, -и	-у, -ю, -мени
Accusative Animate	-а, -я	-а, -я, -ь	-а, -я, -ь
Accusative Inanimate	accusative = nominative	accusative = nominative	accusative = nominative
Instrumental	-ом, -ем	-ой, -ей, ь+ю	о+м, е+м, -менем
Prepositional	Consonant + е, -е	-е, -ии, -и	-е, -и, -мени

RUSSIAN CASES, SUMMARY – PLURAL

Case	Endings		
	Masculine	**Feminine**	**Neutral**
Nominative	-ы, -и	-ы, -и, -ии	-а, -я, -ия
Genitive	Consonant + ов, -ей, -ев	-a removed, -ь, -ий, -ей	-о removed, -ий, -ей
Dative	-ам, -ям		
Accusative Animate	Consonant + ов, -ев, -ей	-a removed, -ь, -ий, -ей	accusative = nominative
Accusative Inanimate	accusative = nominative	accusative = nominative	
Instrumental	-ами, -ями		
Prepositional	-ах, -ях		

THE GENITIVE CASE OF COUNTRY AND CITY NAMES

Country name ends in	The ending is changed to	Example
Hard consonant	а	Сингапу**р** – из Сингапур**а** Singapore – from Singapore
й	я	Уругва**й** – из Уругва**я** Uruguay – from Uruguay
я, ь	и	Итали**я** – из Итали**и** Italy – from Italy
а	ы	Москв**а** – из Москв**ы** Moscow – from Moscow

LANGUAGE NAMES VOCABULARY LIST

Initial form – по + language name + ск	English version
русский – по-русски	Russian – in Russian
английский – по-английски	English – in English
немецкий – по-немецки	German – in German
французский – по-французски	French – in French
испанский – по-испански	Spanish – in Spanish
итальянский – по-итальянски	Italian – in Italian
норвежский – по-норвежски	Norwegian – in Norwegian
шведский – по-шведски	Swedish – in Swedish
финский – по-фински	Finnish – in Finnish
украинский – по-украински	Ukrainian – in Ukrainian
польский – по-польски	Polish – in Polish
турецкий – по-турецки	Turkish – in Turkish

VERB CONJUGATION IN THE PRESENT TENSE

All the verbs are divided into the 1st and 2nd conjugation.

1st conjugation verbs:

1) All the verbs that end in **-ать**, except these four: **гнать (chase), держать (hold), слышать (hear), дышать (breathe)** that belong to the 2nd conjugation.

Игр**ать** (play) – Я игра**ю** (I play) – 1st conjugation
Слышать (hear) – Я слыш**у** (I hear) – 2nd conjugation

2) All the verbs that end in **-ять, -уть, -ють, -ыть, -чь**

Гул**ять** (walk) – Я гуля**ю** (I walk)
М**ыть** (wash) – Я мо**ю** (I wash)

3) All the verbs that end in '**-еть**', except for **терпеть (bear, suffer), вертеть (spin), обидеть (offend), ненавидеть (hate), зависеть (depend), смотреть (watch),** and **видеть (see).**

Бол**еть** (To be sick) – Я боле**ю** (I am sick)

4) Two verbs that end in '**-ить**': **брить (shave, transitive)** and **стелить** (spread, lay, in the context of a tablecloth or bed linen)
Бр**ить** (Shave) – Я бре**юсь** (I shave)

To form the verb in the present tense, remove '**-ть**' from the infinitive and add the corresponding ending.

PRESENT TENSE ENDINGS FOR THE 1ST CONJUGATION

Pronoun/Person	Ending	Example
Я (1st person singular)	-ю	Я игра**ю**. – I play. Я гуля**ю**. – I walk.
Ты (2nd person singular)	-ешь	Ты игра**ешь**. – You play. Ты гуля**ешь**. – You walk.
Он, она, оно (3rd person singular)	-ет	Она игра**ет**. – She plays. Он гуля**ет**. – He walks.
Мы (1st person plural)	-ем	Мы игра**ем**. – We play. Мы гуля**ем**. – We walk.
Вы (2nd person plural)	-ете	Вы игра**ете**. – You play. Вы гуля**ете**. – You walk.
Они (3rd person plural)	-ют	Они игра**ют**. – They play. Они гуля**ют**. – They walk.

2nd conjugation verbs

1) All the verbs that end in **-ить**, except **брить (shave)** and **стелить (spread, lay)**.

Говор**ить** (talk) – Я говор**ю** (I talk)

2) The seven **-еть** verbs: **терпеть (bear, suffer), вертеть (spin), обидеть (offend), ненавидеть (hate), зависеть (depend), смотреть (watch), видеть (see).**

Смотреть (watch) – Я смотрю (I watch)

3) The four **-ать** verbs: **гнать (chase), держать (hold), слышать (hear), дышать (breathe).**

Держать (hold) – Она держ**ит.**

To form the verb in the present tense, remove the three final letters from the infinitive and add the corresponding ending.

PRESENT TENSE ENDINGS FOR THE 2nd CONJUGATION

Pronoun/Person	Ending	Example
Я (1st person singular)	-ю	Я говор**ю**. – I talk. Я смотр**ю**. – I watch.
Ты (2nd person singular)	-ишь	Ты говор**ишь**. – You talk. Ты смотр**ишь**. – You watch.
Он, она, оно (3rd person singular)	-ит	Она говор**ит**. – She talks. Он смотр**ит**. – He watches.
Мы (1st person plural)	-им	Мы говор**им**. – We talk. Мы смотр**им**. – We watch.
Вы (2nd person plural)	-ите	Вы говор**ите**. – You talk. Вы смотр**ите**. – You watch.
Они (3rd person plural)	-ят	Они говор**ят**. – They talk. Они смотр**ят**. – They watch.

Pay attention to the spelling rules:

When the stem of the verb (the verb without the ending) ends in **к, г, х, ж, ш, щ, ч, ц,** it should never be followed by **ю** or **я** and they should be replaced with **у** and **а** respectively.

Example:

У**ч**ить (teach) – Я уч**у** – Они уч**а**т
Ды**ш**ать (breathe) – Дыш**у** – Они дыш**а**т

Also note that **vowel 'e' is replaced with 'ё'** when it becomes stressed in a verb ending.

Example:

Петь – Мы поём (we sing)

Irregular verbs. Unlike in English, there are not many completely irregular verbs in Russian that don't follow any pattern. They should just be memorized. They include:

1) Хотеть (want):
Я хочу, ты хочешь, он/она хочет, мы хотим, вы хотите, они хотят

2) Бежать (run)
Я бегу, ты бежишь, он/она бежит, мы бежим, вы бежите, они бегут

3) Дать (give)
Я даю, ты даёшь, он/она даёт, мы даём, вы даёте, они дают

4) Есть (eat)

Я ем, ты ешь, он/она ест, мы едим, вы едите, они едят

Partially irregular verbs mostly deal with a consonant shift and often involve a certain pattern.

1) '-ова' is replaced by **'у'** + the corresponding ending.

Рис**ова**ть (Paint) – Я рис**у**ю, ты рис**у**ешь (I paint, you paint)
Note that many **'-ова'** verbs are of foreign origin and are easy to understand and memorize.
Игнорировать – To ignore
Тестировать – To test
Регистрировать – To register
Организовать – To organize
Программировать – To program

2) +е between consonants
Брать (take) – Я б**е**ру, ты б**е**рёшь (I, you take)

3) х turns into **д**
Е**х**ать (go by vehicle) – Я е**д**у, они е**д**ут (I, they go)

4) д is replaced with **ж** for **'я'**
Видеть (see) – Я вижу (I see)

5) т is replaced with **в**
Жить (live) – Я живу, ты живёшь, она живёт, вы живёте, мы живём, они живут

6) е is replaced with **о**
Петь (sing) – Я пою, она поёт (I sing, she sings)

7) с is replaced with **ш**
Писать (write) – Я пишу, мы пишем (I write, we write)

DEMONSTRATIVE PRONOUNS

Just like in English, Russian demonstrative pronouns point out a person or an object that is close to or far from the speaker. The initial forms 'этот' and 'тот' coincide with the English 'this' and 'that'.

From the grammatical point of view, demonstrative pronouns correspond to the related noun in number, gender, and case, which makes them very similar to adjectives.

ЭТОТ – ЭТИ / THIS – THESE

Case	Singular			Plural
	Masculine	**Feminine**	**Neutral**	
Nominative	Этот	Эта	Это	Эти
Genitive	Этого	Этой	Этого	Этих
Dative	Этому	Этой	Этому	Этим
Accusative	Этот (inanimate) Этого (animate)	Эту	Этот (inanimate) Этого (animate)	Эти (inanimate) Этих (animate)
Instrumental	Этим	Этой	Этим	Этими
Prepositional	Этом	Этой	Этом	Этих

ТОТ – ТЕ / THAT – THOSE

Case	Singular			Plural
	Masculine	**Feminine**	**Neutral**	
Nominative	Тот	Та	То	Те
Genitive	Того	Той	Того	Тех
Dative	Тому	Той	Тому	Теми
Accusative	Тот (inanimate) Того (animate)	Ту	Тот (inanimate) Того (animate)	Те (inanimate) Тех (animate)
Instrumental	Тем	Той	Тем	Теми
Prepositional	Том	Той	Том	Тех

Example:

Мне не нравится **эта** юбка. – I don't like **this** skirt.

Пожалуйста, дайте мне **тот** сыр. – Please, give me **that** cheese.

Тебя нравятся **эти** брюки? – Do you like **these** pants?

ANSWER KEY
UNIT I

EXERCISE 1

Conversation 1

A: Привет!

B: Привет!

A: Как дела?

B: Хорошо. А у тебя?

A: И у меня.

Conversation 2

A: Здравствуйте!

B: Добрый день!

A: Как Ваши дела?

B: Спасибо, хорошо! А как Вы?

A: Я тоже хорошо!

Conversation 3

A: Привет! Как жизнь?

B: Привет! Отлично! А ты как?

A: Спасибо, хорошо!

Conversation 4

A: Доброе утро!

B: Доброе утро!

A: Как Вы?

B: Спасибо, неплохо! А Вы?

A: Я тоже!

EXERCISE 2

1) дедушка

2) бабушка

3) папа

4) мама

5) тётя

6) дядя

7) двоюродный брат

8) двоюродная сестра

EXERCISE 3

не женат – not married (about males)	женат – married
студент – student (male)	студентка –student (female)
сестра – sister	брат – brother
мама и папа – mom and dad	родители – parents
его зовут – his name is	её зовут – her name is
парень – guy, young man	девушка – girl, young woman
дети – children, kids	ребёнок – child, kid
не замужем – not married (about females)	замужем – married
один друг – one friend	друзья – friends
племянник – nephew	племянница – niece
внук и внучка – grandson and granddaughter	внуки – grandchildren
двоюродный брат – cousin (male)	двоюродная сестра –cousin (female)
дядя – uncle	тётя – aunt
мужчина – man	woman – женщина
друг – male friend	подруга – female friend
сын – son	дочка – daughter

EXERCISE 4

1) Меня зовут – My name is

2) Её зовут – Her name is

3) Его зовут – His name is

4) У меня есть – I have

5) У них есть – They have

6) Мне двадцать три года – I'm twenty-three years old

7) Ей двадцать один год – She's twenty-one years old

8) Ему двадцать семь лет – He's twenty-seven years old

EXERCISE 5

1) Their names are Nastya and Olya – B

2) Our names are Masha and Sveta – A

3) Your names are Bogdan and Valera – C

4) Your name is Igor Vladimirovich – E

5) Your name is Vera – D

EXERCISE 6

1) G   **5)** C

2) D   **6)** H

3) E   **7)** A

4) B   **8)** F

EXERCISE 7

1) её

2) их

3) его

4) их

5) её

6) их

7) его

8) его

EXERCISE 8

1) Я архитектор. – I'm an architect.

2) Он водитель. – He's a driver.

3) Они друзья. – They are friends.

4) Вы профессор. – You are a professor.

5) Она учительница. – She's a teacher.

6) Он продавец. – He's a shop assistant.

7) Он пилот. – He's a pilot.

8) Она художница. – She is a painter.

9) Ты юрист. – You are a lawyer.

EXERCISE 9

1) его

2) тебя

3) их

4) её

5) вас

6) их

7) вас

8) Вас

EXERCISE 10

1) У нас есть сестра.

2) У него есть жена.

3) У вас есть дети.

4) У него есть бабушка.

5) У вас есть сын.

6) У неё есть подруга.

7) У них есть племянница.

8) У нас есть дом.

9) У меня есть собака.

10) У тебя есть дочка.

EXERCISE 11

1) ей

2) мне

3) им

4) нам

5) тебе

6) ему

7) вам

8) тебе

9) ей

10) вам

EXERCISE 12

1) Мне тридцать четыре года.

2) Нам двадцать лет.

3) Ему сорок пять лет.

4) Ей пятьдесят один год.

5) Тебе шестьдесят девять лет.

6) Им пять лет.

7) Ей сто три года.

8) Вам шестнадцать лет.

9) Мне семьдесят лет.

10) Ему восемьдесят четыре года.

EXERCISE 13

1) ей/dance

2) мне/jog

3) им/sing

4) тебе/draw

5) ему/sing

6) вам/play the guitar

7) нам/travel

8) мне/swim

9) вам/play football

10) тебе/ride a bike

EXERCISE 14

1) C – твоя

2) A – её

3) D – наша

4) G – ваш

5) B – их

6) F – моя

7) H – его

8) E – наш

EXERCISE 15

1) 1 – C – b

2) 2 – A – d

3) 3 – D – a

4) 4 – E – e

5) 5 – B – c

EXERCISE 16

I	II	III	IV	V
1) c	**1)** a	**1)** b	**1)** e	**1)** d
2) g	**2)** f	**2)** h	**2)** i	

EXERCISE 17

Conversation 1

A: Привет!

B: Привет! Как тебя зовут?

A: Меня зовут Вика.

B: Очень приятно! А меня зовут Степан.

A: Откуда ты?

B: Я из России. А ты?

A: Я из Украины. Сколько тебе лет?

B: Мне двадцать один год. А тебе?

Conversation 2

A: У тебя есть семья?

B: Да, у меня есть семья. У меня есть сестра Лена.

A: Сколько ей лет?

B: Ей тридцать четыре года.

A: Откуда она?

B: Она из России.

A: У неё есть семья?

B: Да, она замужем.

Conversation 3

A: Здравствуйте!

B: Здравствуйте! Как Вас зовут?

A: Меня зовут Валерий Петрович.

B: Сколько Вам лет?

A: Мне сорок лет.

B: Кто Вы по профессии?

A: Я врач.

EXERCISE 18

Text 1

1) меня

2) мне

3) из

4) учительница

5) испанский

6) по-русски

7) замужем

8) ему

9) Аргентины

10) зовут

11) нас

12) лет

13) есть

14) его

15) пять

16) мы

Text 2

1) зовут	**5)** моя	**9)** девушка	**13)** их
2) года	**6)** её	**10)** мой	
3) на	**7)** ему	**11)** его	
4) замужем	**8)** по-английски	**12)** меня	

Text 3

1) моя	**4)** танцевать	**7)** своя
2) России	**5)** есть	**8)** его
3) нам	**6)** женат	**9)** нравится

EXERCISE 19

	Лера	Франц	Костя	Грег
студент(ка)	✓			
продавец				✓
актёр		✓		
водитель			✓	
плавать	✓			
рисовать				✓
играть в футбол			✓	
путешествовать		✓		
женат			✓	✓
замужем				
не женат		✓		
не замужем	✓			
есть дети			✓	
нет детей	✓	✓		✓
из россии	✓		✓	
из германии		✓		
из америки				✓
по-русски	✓		✓	✓
по-немецки		✓		
по-английски	✓			✓
по-турецки		✓		

EXERCISE 20

A) Её зовут Жули Решар. Ей восемнадцать лет. Она из Франции. Она студентка. Она говорит по-английски и по-французски. Она не замужем. У неё нет детей.

B) Его зовут Рикардо Феллини. Ему двадцать семь лет. Он из Италии. Он юрист. Он говорит по-английски и по-итальянски. Он женат. У него есть дети.

UNIT II

EXERCISE 1

1) C
2) E
3) G
4) B

5) D
6) A
7) H
8) F

EXERCISE 2

1) Дом родителей
2) Начальник коллеги
3) Деньги мужа
4) Машина племянницы

5) Книги студентов
6) Братья друга
7) Учитель детей
8) Жена брата

EXERCISE 3

1) Это дом твоих родителей.
2) Это начальник их коллеги.
3) Это деньги её мужа.
4) Это машина его племянницы.

5) Это книги наших студентов.
6) Это братья моего друга.
7) Это учитель ваших детей.
8) Это жена моего брата.

EXERCISE 4

1) времени
2) детей
3) братьев, сестёр
4) врачей
5) начальника

6) денег
7) воды
8) людей
9) мужей
10) отдыха

EXERCISE 5

Conversation I: нет, не, не, нет
Conversation II: нет, нет, не, не
Conversation III: нет, нет, не, нет

Conversation IV: ни … ни, нет, не, не, не
Conversation V: нет, не, не, нет, не, нет

EXERCISE 6

1) Нет, у меня нет сестры.
2) Нет, я не говорю по-испански.
3) Нет, я не замужем/женат.
4) Нет, у меня нет детей.
5) Нет, мне не нравится играть в футбол.
6) Нет, у меня нет машины.
7) Нет, мне не нравится моя работа.
8) Нет, у меня не много свободного времени вечером.
9) Нет, мой рабочий день начинается не в семь утра.
10) Нет, мои дети не добираются до школы на автобусе.

EXERCISE 7

1) C

2) F

3) H

4) G

5) B

6) D

7) E

8) A

EXERCISE 8

1) жене

2) моим родителям

3) друзьям

4) моей подруге

5) твоей дочери

6) маме

7) детям

8) моему мужу

9) коллегам

10) твоей сестре

11) людям

12) его брату

EXERCISE 9

1) Маше нравится ходить в походы.

Masha likes to go hiking.

2) Андрею не нравится заниматься садом.

Andrey doesn't like working in the garden.

3) Антону нравится кататься на велосипеде.

Anton likes riding a bike.

4) Марине нравится изучать иностранные языки.

Marina likes learning foreign languages.

5) Наташе не нравятся фильмы ужасов.

Natasha doesn't like horror films.

6) Вике нравится заниматься йогой.

Vika likes doing yoga.

7) Степану не нравится ходить на экскурсии.

Stepan doesn't like going on excursions.

8) Лере не нравится играть в шахматы.

Lera doesn't like playing chess.

9) Милане нравится играть на скрипке.

Milana likes playing the violin.

10) Богдану нравится путешествовать.

Bogdan likes traveling.

EXERCISE 11

1) работу

2) твою сестру

3) музыку

4) завтрак

5) мотоцикл

6) твоего друга

7) тётю

8) нашу столовую

9) мою подругу

10) детей

11) книги

12) её мужа

13) школу

14) еду

EXERCISE 13

1) вечером

2) медсестрой

3) уборкой

4) политикой

5) пилотом

6) собаками

7) утром

8) своей дочерью

9) балетом

10) спортом

11) твоим ключом

12) друзьями

EXERCISE 14

1) Моих друзей – юристом

2) Моей дочери – учёным

3) Твоего сына – таксистом

4) Его жены – архитектором

5) Моего друга – переводчицей

6) Вашего друга – стюардессой

7) Твоего мужа – актрисой

8) Моего племянника – строителем

EXERCISE 18

1) гуляет

2) хотят

3) смотрим

4) опаздывает

5) добираешься

6) сидят

7) играет

8) увлекаетесь

9) просыпается

10) ненавидишь

11) рисует

12) бреется

13) засыпаю

14) забирает

EXERCISE 19

1 – E – Моя собака **хочет** гулять утром, днём и вечером.

My dog wants to walk in the morning, in the afternoon, and in the evening.

2 – K – Твои друзья **хотят** проводить выходные вместе.

Your friends want to spend weekends together.

3 – A – Мы с дочерью **хотим** приготовить вкусный ужин.

My daughter and I want to cook a delicious dinner.

4 – M – Ты **хочешь** читать на русском языке.

You want to read in Russian.

5 – F – Её сын **хочет** купить новую игрушку.

Her son wants to buy a new toy.

6 – C – Ты и твой брат **хотите** ходить в кино по субботам.

Your brother and you want to go to the cinema on Saturdays.

7 – L – Я **хочу** засыпать рано.

I want to fall asleep early.

8 – B – Ваша племянница **хочет** заниматься танцами.

Your niece wants to do dance.

9 – J – Наши коллеги **хотят** добираться до работы на машине.

Our colleagues want to get to work by car.

10 – I – Их начальник **хочет** возвращаться домой рано.

Their boss wants to get back home early.

11 – G – Ваши дети **хотят** играть в компьютерные игры.

Your kids want to play computer games.

12 – D – Мой сосед **хочет** поменять работу.

My neighbor wants to change his job.

13 – H – Его кот **хочет** спать весь день.

His cat wants to sleep all day long.

EXERCISE 20

Verb	Ты	Мы	Вы
Просыпаться	Просыпа**ешь**ся	Просыпа**ем**ся	Просыпа**ете**сь
Просматривать	Просматрива**ешь**	Просматрива**ем**	Просматрива**ете**
Умываться	Умыва**ешь**ся	Умыва**ем**ся	Умыва**ете**сь
Ужинать	Ужина**ешь**	Ужина**ем**	Ужина**ете**
Отвечать	Отвеча**ешь**	Отвеча**ем**	Отвеча**ете**
Заниматься	Занима**ешь**ся	Занима**ем**ся	Занима**ете**сь
Выгуливать	Выгулива**ешь**	Выгулива**ем**	Выгулива**ете**
Ходить	Ход**ишь**	Ход**им**	Ход**ите**
Обедать	Обеда**ешь**	Обеда**ем**	Обеда**ете**
Делать	Дела**ешь**	Дела**ем**	Дела**ете**
Встречаться	Встреч**аешь**ься	Встреча**ем**ся	Встреча**ете**сь
Завтракать	Завтрак**аешь**	Завтрака**ем**	Завтрака**ете**
Разговаривать	Разговарив**аешь**	Разговарива**ем**	Разговарива**ете**
Ложиться	Лож**ишь**ся	Лож**им**ся	Лож**ите**сь
Ходить	Ход**ишь**	Ход**им**	Ход**ите**
Делать	Дела**ешь**	Дела**ем**	Дела**ете**

Verb	Он/Она	Они
Просыпаться	Просыпа**ет**ся	Просыпа**ют**ся
Просматривать	Просматрива**ет**	Просматрива**ют**
Умываться	Умыва**ет**ся	Умыва**ют**ся
Ужинать	Ужина**ет**	Ужина**ют**
Отвечать	Отвеча**ет**	Отвеча**ют**
Заниматься	Занима**ет**ся	Занима**ют**ся
Выгуливать	Выгулива**ет**	Выгулива**ют**
Ходить	Ход**ит**	Ход**ят**
Обедать	Обеда**ет**	Обеда**ют**
Делать	Дела**ет**	Дела**ют**
Встречаться	Встреча**ет**ся	Встреча**ют**ся
Завтракать	Завтрака**ет**	Завтрака**ют**
Разговаривать	Разговарива**ет**	Разговарива**ют**
Ложиться	Лож**ит**ся	Лож**ат**ся
Ходить	Ход**ит**	Ход**ят**
Делать	Дела**ет**	Дела**ют**

EXERCISE 21

1) В шесть тридцать (в половину седьмого, в шесть часов тридцать минут) Никита просыпается.

2) В шесть сорок пять (без пятнадцати семь, в шесть часов сорок пять минут) Никита умывается.

3) В семь часов (ровно в семь часов, в семь утра) Никита завтракает.

4) В семь двадцать (в двадцать минут восьмого, в восемь часов двадцать минут) Никита выходит из дома.

5) В восемь (в восемь утра, ровно в восемь, в восемь часов) Никита идёт на совещание.

6) В час тридцать (в половину второго, в час тридцать минут, в тринадцать тридцать) Никита обедает.

7) В пять часов (ровно в пять, в пять часов вечера, в семнадцать часов) Никита заканчивает рабочий день.

8) В шесть десять (в десять минут седьмого, в шесть (восемнадцать) часов десять минут) Никита возвращается домой.

9) В семь часов (в семь часов вечера, ровно в семь, в девятнадцать часов) Никита ужинает.

10) В семь пятьдесят пять (без пяти (минут) восемь, в семь (девятнадцать) часов пятьдесят пять минут) Никита ходит на прогулку.

11) В девять двадцать пять (в девять часов (двадцать один час) двадцать пять минут) Никита смотрит телевизор.

12) В десять тридцать (в половину одиннадцатого, в десять часов тридцать минут, в двадцать два часа тридцать минут) Никита засыпает.

EXERCISE 23

	Маша				
	Ходить в бассейн	**Бегать по утрам**	**Работать из дома**	**Ложиться спать рано**	**Ходить в спортзал**
Часто					
Редко					
Всегда			✓		
Никогда не					
Обычно					
Иногда		✓		✓	
Каждый день					
Раз в неделю	✓				
По вторникам					
По средам					✓

	Сергей и Андрей				
	Ходить в бассейн	**Бегать по утрам**	**Работать из дома**	**Ложиться спать рано**	**Ходить в спортзал**
Часто	✓				
Редко					
Всегда					
Никогда		✓			
Обычно				✓	
Иногда					
Каждый день					✓
Раз в неделю					
По вторникам			✓		
По средам					

Маша, Сергей и Андрей соседи, они разные, но они друзья. Они все занимаются спортом. Им нравится плавание. Сергей и Андрей часто ходят в бассейн, Маша ходит в бассейн раз в неделю. Друзья также ходят в спортзал, Маша – по средам, а Сергей и Андрей каждый день. Но друзьям не нравится бегать по утрам. Сергей и Андрей никогда не бегают, Маша бегает только иногда.

Маша всегда работает из дома, а Сергей и Андрей работают из дома только по вторникам. Маша любит читать и смотреть фильмы и только иногда она ложится спать рано. Сергей и Андрей обычно ложатся спать рано – их рабочий день в офисе начинается в восемь утра.

Masha, Sergey, and Andrey are friends. They all do sports. They like swimming. Sergey and Andrey often go to the swimming pool, Masha goes to the swimming pool once a week. The friends also go to the gym; Masha goes there on Wednesdays and Sergey and Andrey do it every day. But the friends don't like jogging in the morning. Sergey and Andrey never jog, while Masha jogs only sometimes.

Masha always works from home, while Sergey and Andrey work from home only on Tuesdays. Masha likes reading and watching movies and she goes to bed early only sometimes. Sergey and Andrey usually go to bed early—their working day in the office starts at eight o'clock in the morning.

EXERCISE 24

2nd person: ходишь, бегаешь, работаешь, ложишься
1st person: хожу, бегаю, работаю, ложусь

EXERCISE 25

I	II	III
1) в	**1)** в	**1)** к
2) через	**2)** на	**2)** к
3) по	**3)** каждый	**3)** в
4) в	**4)** через	**4)** на
5) в	**5)** по	**5)** около
	6) на	**6)** ко

UNIT III

EXERCISE 1

1) 6
2) 5
3) 13
4) 7

5) 14
6) 12
7) 11
8) 15

9) 10
10) 2
11) 3
12) 9

13) 1
14) 4
15) 8
16) 16

EXERCISE 2

1) между
2) на
3) от

4) в
5) за
6) от

EXERCISE 3

1) Вокзал
2) Школа
3) Аэропорт
4) Библиотека

EXERCISE 5

1) B
2) G
3) C
4) H
5) I

6) D
7) A
8) F
9) J
10) E

EXERCISE 6

1) вход
2) ключ
3) денег
4) прохожего
5) номер

6) кошелёк
7) лифт
8) билет
9) выход
10) карточкой/картой

EXERCISE 7

1) C
2) B/E
3) A

4) F
5) B/E
6) D

EXERCISE 8

1) фотографировали, посещали
2) вызвал
3) переходил

4) паковали
5) спросил (ла), depends on your sex

EXERCISE 9

1) D
2) C
3) A

4) E
5) B

EXERCISE 10

Text 1

1) сажусь
2) еду
3) выхожу

4) сажусь
5) еду
6) ехала

Text 2

1) летел
2) сошёл
3) взял

4) вышел
5) сел
6) вышел

7) вошёл
8) ехал

EXERCISE 12

1) бегу
2) бежит
3) ездим
4) ходят
5) бежит

6) едите
7) иду
8) ходит
9) бежите
10) ездят

EXERCISE 13

1) D
2) F
3) E

4) A
5) B
6) C

EXERCISE 15

1) вернулись
2) приехали
3) наслаждались
4) отель
5) экскурсовод
6) музеи
7) дискотеки
8) достопримечательности

1) путешествие
2) багаж
3) аэропорту
4) взял
5) за
6) кошелёк
7) денег
8) администратор
9) номера

UNIT IV

PART I

EXERCISE 3

1) D	**5)** C
2) G	**6)** E
3) A	**7)** B
4) H	**8)** F

EXERCISE 4

1) У моей подруги длинные, густые (густые, длинные) волосы.

2) Мне не нравится моя внешность.

3) Какого цвета волосы у Вашей мамы?

4) У моего мужа нет бороды.

5) У твоего парня голубые или карие (карие или голубые) глаза?

6) Сколько весит твой кот?

7) Она говорит, что у неё большие уши.

8) У мужчины был толстый подбородок.

EXERCISE 5

A) Её зовут Марина. Ей двадцать пять лет. Её рост – сто семьдесят пять сантиметров. Она высокая. Она весит восемьдесят семь килограмм. У неё зелёные глаза. У неё короткие, вьющиеся волосы. Она блондинка. У неё длинные ресницы и тонкие пальцы.

B) Его зовут Арсений. Ему сорок лет. Его рост сто шестьдесят девять сантиметров. Он весит шестьдесят пять килограмм. У него голубые глаза и короткие, прямые волосы. У него нет бороды. У него тонкие губы.

EXERCISE 6

1) В прошлом году твоя мама была полная. Сейчас она стройная.

2) В двадцать лет у моего брата были густые волосы. Сейчас он лысый.

3) В детстве у ваших детей были светло-русые волосы. Сейчас они тёмно-русые.

4) В пятнадцать лет у меня были вьющиеся волосы. Сейчас у меня прямые волосы.

5) В школе наш дядя был очень высокий. Сейчас он среднего роста.

EXERCISE 7

1) D

2) A

3) C

4) B

PART II

EXERCISE 1

1) B   **4)** D
2) E   **5)** A
3) C   **6)** F

EXERCISE 2

1) F	**5)** B
2) E	**6)** C
3) A	**7)** D
4) H	**8)** G

EXERCISE 3

	Достоинство	Недостаток	Нравится в людях	Не нравится в людях
Лена	креативная	лень	честность	злые
Саша	трудолюбивый	капризный	энергичные	глупые
Дима	ответственный	скучный	весёлые	ленивые
Настя	добрая	раздражительная	романтичные	лентяи/ленивые

PART III

EXERCISE 1

1) – I   **3)** – G   **5)** – D   **7)** – B   **9)** – F
2) – C   **4)** – A   **6)** – E   **8)** – J   **10)** – H

EXERCISE 3

1) солнечный   **3)** погода   **5)** будет идти   **7)** минус   **9)** душно
2) шёл   **4)** будет   **6)** было   **8)** идёт   **10)** морозная

EXERCISE 4

1) – D   **3)** – A
2) – C   **4)** – B

EXERCISE 5

1) – C   **3)** – A   **5)** – B   **7)** – D
2) – F   **4)** – H   **6)** – G   **8)** – E

UNIT V

PART I

EXERCISE 3

1) G	**5)** H
2) E	**6)** C
3) A	**7)** B
4) F	**8)** D

EXERCISE 4

Одежда Clothes	Обувь Shoes	Молочные продукты Dairy products	Напитки Beverages	Мясо Meat	Овощи Vegetables	Фрукты Fruits	Крупы и мука Groats and flour
нижнее бельё, платье, штаны, костюм	сапоги, ботинки, туфли	молоко, кефир, йогурт, сметана, сливки	чай, кофе, сок	свинина, курица, сосиски, колбаса, говядина	салат, картофель, лук, помидоры, морковь	ананас, бананы, персики, мандарины, груши	рис, макароны, гречка, батон, хлеб

EXERCISE 5

Only two nouns change their forms in the accusative case

1) Куртку

2) Одежду

EXERCISE 6

1) по

2) килограмм

3) торговом

4) дал

5) кассу

6) литра

7) копейки

8) грамм

9) на

10) супермаркете

11) кассе

12) сдачи

EXERCISE 7

1) купить

2) -

3) покупаешь

4) заплатить

5) платим

6) купила

7) оплатить

8) купить

9) заплатили

10) покупать

EXERCISE 8

1) это
2) ту
3) эти
4) этих
5) те

6) том
7) эти
8) этот
9) те
10) эту

PART II

EXERCISE 1

Попросить меню/счёт, забронировать столик, позвать официанта,
оставить чаевые, пойти в ресторан, попросить счёт

EXERCISE 2

1) заказ (the rest are furniture items)
2) котлета (the rest are cutlery)
3) лапша (the rest are generic names)

4) медленный (the rest describe food, while this one doesn't)
5) отбивная (the rest are plant-based dishes)

EXERCISE 3

1) быстрая
2) медленная
3) хорошее
4) вкусная
5) солёный

6) запечённые
7) сладкие
8) горячая
9) невкусное
10) жареное

EXERCISE 4

1) оформим
2) закажут
3) пойдём
4) купят
5) пойдём

6) закажу
7) поиграем
8) позовем
9) забронируют
10) заплачу

EXERCISE 5

1) F	**5)** H
2) C	**6)** D
3) A	**7)** F
4) B	**8)** G

MORE BOOKS BY LINGO MASTERY

We are not done teaching you Russian until you're fluent!

Here are some other titles you might find useful in your journey of mastering Russian:

✓ Russian Short Stories for Beginners

✓ Intermediate Russian Short Stories

✓ 2000 Most Common Russian Words in Context

✓ Conversational Russian Dialogues

But we got many more!

Check out all of our titles at **www.LingoMastery.com/russian**

Made in the USA
Monee, IL
28 June 2023

37906880R00122